RECALIBRATE

A NEW MEASURE FOR FAMILY MINISTRY

RON HUNTER JR., PH.D.

General Editor

randall house

114 Bush Rd | Nashville, TN 37217
randallhouse.com

Printed in the United States of America

13-ISBN 9781614841067

Table of Contents

Recalibrate the Challenges of Family Ministry

Introduction

The definition of recalibrate is to adjust, shift, or bring in line with a standard. People recalibrate for the purpose of modifying, improving accuracy, reducing errors, and aligning more correctly. In John 13, Jesus helps Peter recalibrate his view of servant-leadership when stooping to wash Peter's feet; Jesus would do it again when commanding Peter to "feed my sheep" after Peter's denial. After Mt. Carmel, while facing an uncertain and depressing future, God asked Elijah to recalibrate and get back in the game. The two bookend passages of Malachi 4:6 and Luke 1:17 both refer to "turning the hearts back," which certainly describes a recalibration. Finally, as God's people entered the promised land, He told them in Deuteronomy 6 to recalibrate generational influences by teaching their kids in the daily moments of everyday life.

Some churches are new to family ministry while others have been at it for awhile. Common phrases today are, "We are new…" or "How do we know if family ministry is working?" Pastors cannot see instant results because developing worldviews and new habits can't be purchased in a box or corrected in a six-week sermon series. Most pastors default to comparing how their churches measure up to others. For decades, maybe centuries, churches tracked attendance and offerings as the two primary metrics with little regard for spiritual health, discipleship, or reaching other generations. No wonder our churches are greying and slowly dying.

Today's ministry leaders know what they want to accomplish and have ideas for growth goals. But many struggle to know if they are on the right track. How do you measure Deuteronomy 6, Ephesians 6, Psalm 78, and numerous other family ministry passages offering principles of generational discipleship? It's easy to understand age-specific ministries like children, youth, college, or adults. But contrast that with a non age-specific category like family ministry and you have very few good models from the last 3-4 decades. Unfamiliar ideas seem vague or just beyond our grasp. If not careful, when people cannot define something, measure, nor cast a clear vision for it, they stop trying to work toward such accomplishments. Recalibration offers clarity to family ministry in a vital look at the future of the church.

Clarity distinguishes people who daydream from those who know how to recalibrate and accomplish big goals. Unless you have a reliable way to measure goals, you can neither lament nor celebrate the journey. People respect what you inspect, but what are you inspecting? As ministry leaders perpetuate unhealthy norms that hurt outcomes, you will discover new discipleship norms that replace poor habits and you will see clear ways to measure that particular goal. Part of your immediate goals should be helping everyone in your congregation feel like part of the church family. Help each person, single or married, who is either a mom, dad, son, or daughter to see how family ministry embraces every part of a church family. Even if that person is a college student, divorced, no kids, or if they are a widow or elderly with no biological family in the church, every person has value as part of the family of God and can confidently minister to others (peers, younger, or older) with a family-like connection.

Fifteen authors joined forces to bring you this book project. Most authors wrote to the ministry leaders in the church while some wrote to parents or grandparents. To help you distinguish the difference, you will see small icons at the start of each chapter that either show a church (ministry leader) or home (parents and grandparents). Overwhelmingly, most church leaders have children, grown or still in the home. As a leader, you strive to model family ministry while teaching it, even imperfectly. You can see why writing to both audiences makes sense.

The authors represent the very best thought leaders on family ministry and each brings expertise in his or her area to help you adjust and measure for healthy outcomes. It's time to stop asking how other churches are doing family ministry and ask, "How should my church do family ministry?" It's time to recalibrate. Help your parents and grandparents see their role in a whole new light. Teach parents to truly connect on a deeper level with their kids. Empower volunteers and staff to think differently about events at church and the ways they carry over into everyday life. Examine how children's, youth, and college ministry fits within family ministry while maintaining their distinctiveness. This book helps you see family ministry from 14 distinct areas of your church, enables you to spot unhealthy norms, offers new norms, and most importantly provides ways to measure each area.

Ron Hunter Jr., Ph.D.
Founder of D6
Co-Founder of the D6 Conference
Executive Director & CEO of Randall House

RE**CALIBRATE**
the Big Picture

1
Creating a Discipleship Culture for the Family

Philip Nation

The word "family" brings varying images to mind. Some are joyful while others are painful. Family holds us together and sometimes it drives us mad. But no matter how we feel about family, it's often the fountainhead for our spiritual condition.

My family history involves Christian parents who actively led my sister and me to faith in Christ. We were involved in church from my earliest memories. Mom and Dad were supportive when I felt called to full-time ministry and when my sister's husband did the same. My wife Angie and I worked to create a disciple-making environment for our sons, Andrew and Chris. Congregational activities have been standard, and we introduced biblical learning intentionally throughout their childhood.

Seeing my boys become Christians and faithfully following Jesus has been our highest priority. But that is easier typed in a chapter than done. You and I both know that setting up a discipling culture in family life—for church leaders or members—is a constant struggle. But it is what we're called to do; for ourselves and in the service of others.

Proverbs 6:23 (CSB) teaches, "For a command is a lamp, teaching is a light, and corrective discipline is the way to life." Imagine discipleship as a way of life for the families of your church. Rather than the spiritual deterioration from selfishness, there is godliness.

Rather than the assault of worldly wisdom, there is biblical thinking. Your leadership can bring about a gospel-focus that creates healthy family discipleship.

Your help to families will be like a doctor administering an immunization against disease. Healthy church leadership aids families in building resistance to spiritual illness. It recalibrates them from infection to good health.

The way forward is for you to do three things. First, you need to tell the truth about the spiritual condition in families today. Second, you need to offer practices that will develop a healthy disciple-making culture in the home. Finally, set reasonable measurements to know if families are embracing a discipling culture in the home. I am confident that you can recalibrate families to embrace a healthy disciple-making environment.

Current Unhealthy Norms

Too many families live with unhealthy spiritual patterns. One question you may ask is: *Do they even know it?* The answer is yes and no. Many operate blissfully unaware of it all. They float in and out of church programming with nods of affirmation regarding the importance of discipleship but they simply don't realize their own role. Some are painfully aware that spiritual disorder plagues their homes. But no matter their level of understanding, the norm for families is living with spiritual diseases. To know what to do, first we must understand the issues. Let's investigate a few common diseases.

Spiritual Absentia. Family members live with each other but meaningful relationships are missing. As the calendars fill up, parents move into survival mode. Children move into gratification mode. Everyone works for the good of their own emotions and relational chasms are formed. At the core, family members are absent.

The absence happens in all three realms of life. Physically, they are not in the same room very often. The round-robin tournament feel to the dinner table quietly announces that no one is ever actually together, except for the car rides to here and there. Emotionally, family members drift from each other or even build barriers against one another. Parents frustrated with their kids grow tired of being spurned. Kids, weary of nagging parents, shut down. People talk but don't connect.

The worst part of all is the spiritual absenteeism. Parents don't spiritually connect with their kids. Surface-tension religious conversations occur about "what you learned in Sunday School" or "Did you have fun at church today?" Parents hold their spiritual concern for kids as an almost secretive portion of their lives. Discipleship happens but not by anyone in the family. Instead, parents act as surrogates hoping the leaders of the church will disciple their children. But, as a leader, you cannot undo in three hours what the world does to that child or teenager for the remaining six days and 21 hours in each week. The *Spiritual Absentia* of parents creates a void that their grown child will have to fill in another season of life.

Hobbyism. The issues that actually create presence and conversation are the exercises invented to be diversions from the serious portions of life. The reversal of fortune on families' attention is staggering. Rather than discipling kids on the issues of faith, families invest small fortunes and enormous time commitments to the tools of entertainment.

Rather than discipling one another to become dependent upon Christ, we create leeches of leisure. Kids are taught to excel academically, be proficient in the arts, enjoy a pastime, or master a sport so they will be happy adults.

Their schedule revolves around the next external activity that feeds the ego rather than humbling the spirit. The tools of our entertainment become the masters of family life. They are terrible masters that set faith-building to the side in favor of worldly pursuits. By surrendering family life to *Hobbyism*, parents disciple kids to believe that entertainment is the point of life. They create the worst kind of church attender—a consumer of religious goods and services rather than a servant of Christ and His mission.

Selective Subject Syndrome. Since families live under the same roof, they are forced to talk with one another. But the subject of those conversations is generally under the control of the parents. *Selective Subject Syndrome* allows parents to avoid difficult subjects. Reluctance takes the place of intentional discipleship because the issues of the day are awkward and embarrassing to navigate. Mom and Dad simply scoot by them to the easier discussions. In doing so, the family avoids the messy issues that would lead to a deeper walk with Jesus.

One reason for the existence of this disease is the limited time family members have with one another. Because of *Hobbyism* and overworked parents, conversation time has decreased significantly. Mornings are spent getting ready for the day's packed schedule. Drive time is spent with everyone looking at a digital screen. Evenings are for doing homework and settling everyone into bed. The only hope is the weekend but it is consumed with extracurricular activities and the mythical "down time" hoped for by weary parents.

Rather than prioritizing conversations with our family members, our busy schedules squeeze out any relational time. With such short moments for actual dialogue, they opt for the shallow subjects that maintain a familial connection. Problems and secrets are tolerated in the hopes that we will get to them "at the appropriate time." The changing social norms go undiscussed because "there is not enough time to get into that right now." Every discussion that could lead to a deeper life of discipleship is postponed. Our talks are kept in check; and so is any spiritual growth.

Secularization. Families also allow worldly wisdom to guide decision making; especially for their youngsters. In the face of *Selective Subject Syndrome*, kids are left on their own to find answers. If you don't provide a safety net of robust discipleship through church ministries, there is only one place left to get advice: the world.

Tragically, it is sometimes celebrated. When a family member takes time to think through a problem (job change, relationship, financial decision), conventional thinking is lauded as the answer. Bible study is seldom engaged when it should be the go-to source for wisdom. The disease starts in the thinking process and bears fruit in ungodly behavior. The world screams for the attention of undiscipled teenagers, and parents inadvertently teach kids to take the path of least resistance. The end result is that the sacred is sacrificed on the altar of selfish living.

Romanticism. Families dream of an easy life where the rainbows happen without the interruption of an actual storm. The *Romanticism* disease is the misplaced desire for life to be all about comfort and safety. Parents push for a real-life daydream to take hold of kids' lives so hurts are avoided and heartbreak never visits.

The disease even has a religious form. Promises of a life of meaning are replaced with promises of happiness. Jesus is a sanctified Santa Claus who brings gifts to people who are good, or a Cosmic Traffic Cop tasked with keeping life moving with minimal fender-benders. Personal ease becomes the end goal of it all. When the mission of God requires sacrifice and the loss of comfort, Christ's lordship is rejected because it involves difficulty. The false form of discipleship is more focused on the disciple than on the Lord of the disciple.

Before you can set a new standard, you must tell the truth about these unhealthy norms in family life. And, let's be honest...you know these are the norms. They are not the rare outliers. These diseases are the default dispositions of defective discipleship. Though seemingly catastrophic, you can recalibrate families and ministry for effective disciple making.

Recalibrate to a New Norm

Unhealthy families float in and out of Bible study groups and worship services with no indications of real spiritual growth. Once you are willing to face the anemic condition they live in, you can cast a new vision for them to embrace. As their leader, you can recalibrate their thinking and behavior to a new norm.

The Pastoral Epistle of 2 Timothy gives deep insight into Paul's disciple-making desires for Timothy and the church. Though it does not directly address family life, the letter does reveal a principle for your leadership in discipling families.

In 2 Timothy 2:2 (CSB), Paul wrote, *"What you have heard from me in the presence of many witnesses, commit to faithful men who will be able to teach others also."* Timothy was not to tackle the whole of Kingdom work on his own. Instead, he was to disciple others into healthy leaders who would in turn do the same for others. We are called to be disciples who make other disciples. You can set this as a powerful new norm for families. The spiritual work of a family is to raise disciple-making disciples that focus heart, soul, mind, and strength on loving God and living as Kingdom ambassadors.

The influences of the world and the flesh give them sinful skillfulness at relational disconnect and weak-willed behavior modification to create nice people. But isn't the work of the church and discipleship in the family more than just raising courteous kids? Other religions, government, and even superhero movies can teach kids to be mannerly. Your work is to create a multiplying discipleship environment in the church and home. Here are some ways to set up the recalibration.

Tell a better story. Families live in survival mode. Problems in the world and tension in the home conspire to keep family members as friendly combatants with one another. Parents just want peace and quiet (with an emphasis on the quiet). Meanwhile, kids and teenagers treat the home like a catering service that shields them from the rigors of the world. But you can tell them a better story.

Each family in your church has been told a story by the world—and sometimes by congregational leaders—that just getting by in this crazy world is all it takes. Parents are told to raise their children to be mannerly Christians and everything will work out fine. Kids are told to mind their parents' instructions and everything will work out fine. It's as if leaders have handed a script for a living play to families and assigned their parts. The family members are doing their best to fill those "roles" but then…nothing works out fine. Not knowing what to do, they simply try harder at the roles they've been given.

You must tell a better story to the families under your leadership. They need an adjustment in their perception of one another. In perspective, they need to look at life through the lens of eternity. The old cliché is true: we need to stop using people and valuing things, and start valuing people and using things. You can teach leaders of the family to see one another as having eternal value. If they will view each other this way, a better story will be lived out.

The attitude adjustment and change of perspective recalibrates the story you tell of a family's goal. You're not in the business of therapeutic moralism. Church leaders are not helping parents with behavior modification for kids and students. Rather, we are living in God's great story of redemption where everyone is seen through the mindset of how God makes an eternal impact in them and through

13

them. Give parents and ministry leaders a better story to live in so they can carry out Gospel-focused ministry.

Stop raising children. Your work as a ministry leader is not to help parents raise children. We are preparing young people to follow Christ as Lord and then help others to do the same. You can shift your ministry life away from merely assisting parents in rearing well-mannered children to raising up disciple-making disciples.

You should be tired of the sayings, "Kids are the church of tomorrow," and "Students are the next world changers." These are both false. Kids and students are the disciples of today who can make a powerful impact in seeking revival in the church and spiritual awakening in the culture. Put your full weight into moving toward a disciple-making version of ministry leadership. In leading, you will always be called upon to help Mom and Dad (and all the others rearing children) to navigate difficulties in a boy's behavior or a girl's caustic attitude. But do so in view of how it creates disciples for Jesus; not polite and polished children for public display.

Recalibrate your ministry leadership to focus on children and teens as disciples that multiply rather than small humans to present as trophies for proper parenting. Children's, student, and family ministry in your church can be the flashpoint where families finally get it. You can be the vanguard of disciple-making.

Change formations. All organizations operate with a formation. Businesses have organizational charts. Football teams have defensive and offensive schemes for players. Families have default behavior patterns for chores and relationships (sometimes in that order). Churches have budgets and calendars to accomplish goals. You can lead for something more.

Shift your ministry leadership and goals from a catering formation to an equipping formation. We have lived through decades of church life that served to cater to people's perceived highest needs. Often, it was for religious entertainment of kids with movie nights or lock-ins for the teenagers. (I maintain that lock-ins were invented by Satan, but that is just one man's opinion.) Churches that spend all of their energy catering to the entertainment wants and whims of minors are producing religious consumers for the next generations. At the same time, we are giving in to the basest desires of parents to have "the church" do the spiritual raising of their kids. The "drop off for discipleship" model has not worked and will not work.

When your ministry recalibrates to this new focus, you will still have loads of fun but you will have a point to it all. Rather than just one more basketball league for kids or one more 5th Quarter concert for students, you can ask the right questions about it all.

- How does this activity make Jesus the big deal in the lives of kids?
- What is the spiritual fruit that will come from this program?
- Does this equip parents and their students for healthy spiritual growth together?

These questions and all of the ones you can attach to your family ministries will help you choose the right formation.

Plus, you will impact formation change in the home. By setting a ministry example, you'll set families on the path of moving from the comfort business to Kingdom living. Parents, by loving default, want more than just keeping kids out of harm's way. They want a more comfortable and successful life for the kids than they've had. So, their parenting scheme is to help kids be safe, easy, and achieve the elusive "American Dream." Discipleship is the beautiful interruption to the pablum of worldly success. Recalibrate your leadership to move families out of survivalist tactics and entrepreneurial dreaming to raising global troublemakers for God's kingdom.

Integrate all of life as spiritual. The default position of too many ministries—and thus the families involved—is that there is a "spiritual side" to life. It allows family members to put faith behind the glass pane that reads, "break in case of emergency." Lead the ministry as if there is not a sacred-secular divide. The Bible teaches that Jesus' disciples are living in but should not be formed by this world (see passages like 1 John 2 and John 17). It presents a challenge for our families to find their way. They want to show faithfulness to Jesus but not be heckled by friends. Parents especially wish this for their kids. So, compartmentalization happens.

You can lead them to see that all of life is spiritual. Every relationship and action we take is not a reaction to the world and its standards. Rather, we lead one another as spouses and lead our children to live in response to spiritual truth. For the Christian, all of life's work is done in view of God's work in us. As Paul wrote in Colossians 3:17 (CSB), "And whatever you do, in word or in deed, do everything in the name of the Lord Jesus, giving thanks to God the Father through him." If families recalibrate to think spiritually, they will better disciple kids through the normal paces of life.

In leading ministry from a staff position or in a volunteer position, this is one of your greatest opportunities. By nature, kids and students will want the church to either: a) offer a checklist of dos and don'ts to stay in God's good graces, or b) offer a series of activities to simply keep them entertained. In either case, you can show them the way to thinking about the spiritual implications of every scenario, attitude, and action. Infuse the spiritual nature of life's experiences into how they make decisions so discipleship and missional living is at the forefront of their decision making.

Fulfill the whole Great Commission. As a church leader, it's been too easy for us to overemphasize Matthew 28:19 and somehow leave off Matthew 28:20. We've leaned into making disciples (often simplified to mere "invitationalism") and baptizing people. In verse 20, Jesus leads you to the work of "teaching them to observe everything I have commanded you." We need the recalibration in what it means to really make a disciple. It must be more than moving people barely over the threshold of faith and a one-time public identification with Christ. Leading families to embrace all of Christ's commands for all of their lives (both holistically and chronologically) is some of the greatest work you'll ever do.

To do this, you will have to walk away from a model of behavior modification and factoid transfer as main ministry activities. Instead, create a model of learning that leads to application in real-life circumstances. As a kid, I did Bible Drills in Discipleship Training classes with church. It taught me to find verses and even memorize a few. But I was never taught why any of it mattered. You have the whole field of life in front of each kid, student, and family to lead them to apply the Word rather than mimic a cursory knowledge of it. Obedience is never optional. And Jesus commissions us to lead people to infuse His commands into how we live.

Your leadership in this area sets a standard for how parents and siblings interact at home around the Scriptures. Plus, it gives a path for families to integrate it into their conversations. When parents are honest, they admit to holding little ability about how to disciple kids and students. They're lost in the mire of simply trying to leverage acceptable behavior from the kiddos. In your leadership, give parents the tools to teach how the Word is not to just be heard but obeyed. Do it by recalibrating how you teach to focus on active application. It is how we can make holiness habitual in the lives of parents and their kids.

Teach the young to be disciple makers. Parents have a natural hesitation for unrealistic expectations on their own kids. The idea that their child would disciple others seems...out of reach. They love and are biased toward their own children but being a disciple maker seems an awfully grown-up thing to do. And yet, our family members are filled with the same Holy Spirit and have the same commission as the greatest saints of recent and ancient history. Your ministry will take on new life and power when you recalibrate the expectations of what God can do through families, students, and children.

But you have a reasonable question running through your mind: How? How do you transition previously consumer-focused kids and teenagers into disciple-making disciples? As you would guess, a full answer could consume a chapter, a book, or a series of books. Disciple making is a complex thing. But it is also simple.

In the basic form of leadership, you guide people to prioritize Jesus above every other passion. You teach and train kids, students, and families how Jesus is better than all the vices the world offers and the "virtues" offered by every other religion. In partnership with parents, help kids and students sense the same calling. Disciple-making is not reserved for a select faction of the church. We are all called, regardless of age, to share our faith and lead those in the faith to live it out. Your work as a leader of a ministry or in a classroom is to engender a multiplying mentality in family ministries. Remind parents that their family is included in the mission of God but not the end of the mission of God. They are recipients of God's grace in order to be distributors of it. They are to raise their kids with grace and mercy so the kids will display grace and mercy so others will receive grace and mercy.

You are called to undermine the spiritual maladies plaguing the spiritual health of families and replace them with disciple-making practices that reveal the Gospel at work within us. The choice you have to make is not between pleasing one demographic in the community or a different group in the church. Your choice is between tolerating unhealthy practices of ministry and generating healthy patterns of multiplicative disciple-making. It is the age old choice between pleasing God or man.

Measuring the New Norm

As a leader, your finish line is reached when life in this world is over. But along the way, you can keep the finish line in sight to target the right direction. Since making disciples who make disciples is the end goal of your family ministries, a few mid-course measurements can help you keep steering properly. Let me offer three to consider.

The first is **faithful living.** Within His final instructions that we call The Great Commission (Matthew 28:16-20), Jesus told the disciples to teach others to obey all of His commands. You can gauge the level of personal faithfulness by looking at the commands of Jesus. Your work as a leader is to give biblical instruction that will lead to personal application. As you draw relationally close to the families in your church, do so with an eye toward observing faithful living. Though not exhaustive of all of Jesus' commands, a good place to start is with His teaching from The Sermon on the Mount (Matthew 5-7). Faithful living will display itself in lives characterized by such things are grace-filled relationships, moral holiness, and an increasing faith in God's power. When you see it, celebrate it with them. When it is absent, lovingly disciple families toward Jesus as their first love.

The second is **fruitful service.** When you lead people to obedience of the Word, service follows. The question many ask is whether or not our service is fruitful. For this idea, you can guide parents and their kids away from programmatic busyness. Your leadership should focus on faithfulness that seeks fruitfulness on behalf of God's mission in the world. Ephesians 2:10 teaches that God has prepared good works for us to accomplish after we are "in Christ." Anyone can stay busy. Leaders must measure whether or not the ministry and the families are spiritually fruitful. Fruitfulness comes from extending grace to those who are difficult, serving others' needs when it is inconvenient, and seeing the lost place faith in Christ. Focusing on fruitfulness will guard you from simply filling the calendar with congregational activities and declaring yourselves, your family, and the church to be mature. Instead, inspect the fruit from your ministry and test it according to how we see the church living out the faith in the New Testament.

The third is **followers multiplied.** The ultimate fruit of your leadership is new followers of Jesus. It is not the only measurement, but it is the one that we should most earnestly seek. Through the times of great harvest or apparent barrenness, your goal in ministry must not be reputation building for the kids ministry, increased hipness for the student ministry, or appeasement of parents. The ultimate goal is to increase the number of people following Jesus. As you make it your aim, then this beautiful vision will begin to saturate the lives of families in your church. As they see you raising the banner of multiplying followers of Jesus, they will bring their families into the amazing work of making disciples who make disciples.

Resources to Explore Further

Before I conclude this slightly audacious chapter, allow me to recommend three resources to you.

- Check into the *Foundation 260 Bible Reading Plan* by Robby Gallaty. It is a great plan to get families reading the Bible together.
- I would encourage you to check into my book *Habits for Our Holiness*. It teaches how the spiritual disciplines are for everyday people like us, and how God uses them as tools for our spiritual growth.

- Consider using the *The Jesus Storybook Bible* by Sally Lloyd-Jones. It creates a biblically faithful and highly accessible experience with God's Word for children.

"Creating a discipleship culture for the family" is a powerful promise for either an author to make with a chapter title or for a church leader to make to a church. But your desire to follow Christ will not go unnoticed by our Lord. He sees your deep love for others to follow Him, and His Spirit works on hearts before you even think to show up. Rest in the work that the Spirit is doing and be bold in the knowledge that you are serving His great purpose in the church.

2
Staff and Volunteer Dynamics

Brian Haynes

Well-intended chaos. I walked into yet another hotel and conference center coffee shop and sat down to gather my thoughts between sessions. A pastor, who just a few hours earlier attended one of my breakout seminars on strategic development, observed me sitting alone. He walked toward my table eager to chat so I invited him to sit down. He began to tell me about his church context and his desire to implement a plan to make disciples by equipping parents and grandparents to be disciple makers at home. He conveyed the whiteboard version of his strategy with clarity and ease. I encouraged him in his work. "What a great plan!" I commented. He said, "I thought so too. I only have one problem. After three years of trying, I can't make it work." I listened a bit more. It was not long until I began to notice the same pattern I often identify as the greatest threat to the implementation of any well-designed plan. The problem in this case, and in many scenarios, is disjointed leadership. The presenting dysfunctional issue is team.

Of course, team in every church is unique. There are large paid teams in mega-settings with hundreds of volunteers. More often there are small to medium size teams consisting of a few paid staff and mostly volunteers. In any case, small, medium, large, paid or unpaid, it's the people leading ministry who hold the keys to effective family ministry through the local church. Simply, the people in any sort of leadership role must be on the same page, working the same plan, with the same mission in mind, dreaming the same vision dreams, and operating with aligned values. Typically, and unfortunately, this is not the case in many churches. What is the unhealthy norm though?

Current Unhealthy Norms

Well-intended chaos is a real yet general description of the staff and volunteer dynamics in many churches. People mean well but the chaos is real. If the church leadership is disjointed, likely the families that make up the church will also be disjointed when it comes to discipleship. What causes the chaos? There are five key contributors to the unhealthy norm of well-intended chaos.

Missing mission. Mission answers the question, "What are we doing?" To see the horror in the faces of ministry practitioners is not uncommon when asked the question, "What is your clarified mission as a church?" The reason the question is horrific for pastors and ministry leaders is we all know we should do the hard work of leadership to clarify our mission. The problem is, we have not. It's not usually that the mission is a little bit fuzzy to the people who lead and serve in the church, but the situation is worse. The mission is, for all practical purposes, missing. The consequence is no leader in the church understands with clarity "what" we are doing collectively or how their role as a staff or volunteer leader helps accomplish the mission. No one knows the answer to the question, "What am I doing here?" so everyone is left to determine their own mission. Even only two separate misaligned missions on a team guarantee leaders within the same church will be leading in different directions. It is not a sinister oversight. The lack of mission clarity gives way to the tyranny of the urgent, leaving the church to spin in circles as leaders chase their own version of mission. This stirs the chaos, setting ministry teams on separate paths with different mandates, unintentionally.

Values collision. Values are shared convictions moving leaders, both paid and volunteer, in the same direction. Values tell us "why" we are doing what we are doing. Whenever values do not align, a collision is inevitable. Values are deeper than just shared words or common concepts. They drive and even predict the behavior of a person, the trajectory of their work, and the direction in which he or she will lead. It is absolutely common for ministry leaders to serve together with competing values or opposing values. For example, a leader who deeply values family as the first and best environment for faith training will clash with another who deeply values Sunday School as the first and best environment for disciple making. Aligned values would be preferable, but the unhealthy norm involves values collision in one way or another. We don't usually intend for this to be the case. We assume since we are all Christian, our values will be the same. The problem is, our values differ sending mixed signals to all involved in our ministries.

Strategic calamity. Strategy is a clarified, shared plan answering the question of "how" we are doing what we are doing. Again, it would be nice if most churches took the time to clearly chart a course and develop the steps that should be taken along the way to arrive at a preferable future. Most ministry leaders agree that a church ought to make disciples. But ask any given church how they are making disciples and you will find confusion among the leaders, both paid staff and volunteer. Where there is no shared plan, staff and volunteers will naturally create their own plans designed for specific ministry areas like children's ministry or youth ministry. Each plan will be different. When one church has different discipleship strategies for kids, teenagers, adults, men, women, singles, married couples, senior adults, pre-teens, families, and preschoolers, strategic calamity ensues. In this case, everyone is working hard and going nowhere.

Exasperation is the fruit of such a model and frustratingly, this is commonplace.

Vision fog. Clear vision answers the question of "Where" are we going? Or, "where" is God taking us? With words, vision paints the vivid, hopeful, picture of a preferable future beyond the status quo of today or tomorrow. Vision differs from mission by pointing to the future while mission tells us what we are doing today to realize the vision. Left unclarified, volunteers and staff only have the options to determine their own vision for the ministry areas they serve and lead, or to do nothing. The vision fog sets in and the team begins to separate, each person feeling their own way through the present to the future. The effect on families is null. And, that is the problem.

Staffing decisions. Whether we are hiring paid ministry staff or recruiting volunteer ministry staff, the staffing of our teams involves choices we make about people. What is normative in the church today regarding staffing decisions needs some work. Beyond the issues of shared mission, values, strategy, and vision, we need to get better at choosing the right people for the right places of service. We often settle for what seems easy. More than once and in a well-intended way, I have made a poor decision about a particular person for a particular spot on the team. Why? I was overloaded and in a hurry and rushed. Always, those poor choices about people brought a future chaos. In the church, we like to play it nice. So, when we make a bad staffing decision, we are usually really slow to release a person from their assignment giving the chaos momentum. Surely you have heard it said it is important "to get the right people in the right seats on the bus."[1] This is true if you want the "bus" to go anywhere. Unfortunately, most of us have some staff and volunteers in the right seat on the bus, some in the wrong seat, and some who need to get off the bus altogether. We just keep driving like it's all good, unwilling to make the necessary changes.

Let's admit, this is the unhealthy norm. If we want to make disciples by equipping and ministering to families, we will have to do more than design an amazing family ministry program. We have to recalibrate how we build team and navigate staff and volunteer dynamics.

Recalibrate to a New Norm

Family ministry effectiveness. The coffee shop conversation continued. My pastor friend shared about his associate who served the church faithfully for the last fifteen years. "He's a good guy. I love his family. The problem is, he doesn't value family as a vehicle for discipleship. His method for making disciples is Sunday School, only. He tips his hat to parents as disciple-makers but he does nothing to encourage or equip them. Worse than that, the staff and volunteers on his team have embraced his philosophy. How will we ever see the families of our church make disciples at home in this reality?" "You won't," I said, "While Sunday School is incredibly valuable, it is only one side of the discipleship coin. The other side is home. There is something you can do to *SHIFT* the focus of the team, and hopefully your associate, in a way that will be catalytic for the church and the family."

Staff/Volunteer alignment. Certainly, every reader is facing different team challenges. Whatever your difficulty, from lack of team to a giant dysfunctional team, how can you recalibrate to minister to families? It's going to take some work, a little courage, and a lot of leadership, but you can do this. Here are five areas of leadership work to consider.

Total ministry alignment (For Senior Leaders Especially). Apart from repentant hearts and a reviving move of the Holy Spirit, the great need of the Church of Jesus Christ is leadership willing to align staff, volunteers, and ministries of the church to effectively make disciples. For the sake of family ministry as a lens through which every leader in the church thinks about discipleship, alignment is required. This will mean evaluation of the shared mission, values, strategy, and vision. Perhaps the student ministry has a mission statement and a vision that is different from an antiquated or non-existing overall church mission. Possibly different ministries of the church have different strategies or are operating with conflicting values. It is time to recalibrate and align all of it.

While everyone can participate, the catalysts for this kind of work are only senior leaders. A senior pastor, the elders, a church council or leadership team; these are the people who initiate such an alignment effort. If I had a dollar for every time I listen to a youth minister, children's pastor, or a key volunteer wishing for senior leadership who would "make it happen," college tuition would not be an issue for our three girls. Men and women in senior leadership, it is time to own the mantle of leadership.

In every church, even ours, realignment has to occur to ensure the team is effectively pulling in the same direction. Often realignment takes months as we collaborate with leadership, both paid and volunteer, in a process to clarify our mission, values, strategy, and vision. A large goal of our strategic planning is to align every person serving in any way in our ministry for total unity. This ensures we are walking the same path making mission accomplishment likely and realizing our vison a possibility. While the purpose of this chapter is not to teach you the mechanics of missional alignment, it is the first and best step in getting your staff and volunteers on the same page for fruitful family ministry.[2]

Hire or recruit at the values level. Hiring paid staff or recruiting volunteer staff needs to begin at the values level. Let's specifically look at two values (of the five at our church) illustratively. You will plug your own values into this process. Remember a value answers the "why" question for a church or ministry and it also answers the "why" for a person. The goal is to recruit people for the team that already demonstrate aligned values with the church or ministry.

Value 1. Gospel Transformation—Life transformation as a result of receiving and applying the gospel of Jesus Christ.

Recruiting team members at the values level requires time and conversation. For a prospective paid staff member, we would call this an interview process. But what about volunteers? Likely you realize volunteer leaders have the most consistent and direct ministry with the families we seek to minister among. Why wouldn't we interview them too? Beginning at the values level means we ask questions to determine alignment before we bring a team member on board in any role. Our church values gospel transformation. We want to see real life change as a result of people receiving and applying the gospel. Particularly we want to see this take place within the family. Interviewing anyone from an associate pastor to a preschool Sunday School volunteer will involve questions of value like the following:

- Tell us about how your life has been transformed by the gospel of Jesus Christ.
- Describe the last time you offered the gospel to someone and how did you share it?
- If you have children or grandchildren, what do you do in the context of your family life to help them understand the gospel?
- How do you demonstrate the gospel at home?

The answers to these questions will begin to reveal a prospective team member's level of value for gospel transformation. In a preliminary way, we discover behavior that demonstrates alignment with our values. Verifying such alignment is a second step. Learning what others say about the person's behavior as it demonstrates gospel transformation as a value gives us an even clearer picture of alignment before we ever offer a person a place on the team. If we want to see gospel transformation in the church and through the home, onboarding people already driven by such a value is important.

Value 2. Kingdom Partnerships—Partnerships forged for the expansion of the Kingdom of Jesus Christ.

This is a critical value. In fact, this value is what obliterates the silo concept of on-campus ministry and pushes faith into the home. If a potential staff member has this value, he or she will consider all potential partnerships to expand the kingdom by making disciples. The Bible teaches and sociological studies support the idea that the family is the single most important construct in a person's life.

> *Contrary to popular misguided cultural stereotypes and frequent parental misperception, we believe the evidence clearly shows that the single most important social influence on the religious and spiritual lives of adolescents is their parents.*[3]

Understanding the importance of family of origin will lead a team member who values kingdom partnerships and gospel transformation to recognize the most crucial kingdom partnership for the sake of gospel transformation is the close association of church and home.

You get the idea. If we hire or recruit at the values level to begin with, we realize greater unity along the way. Beyond that, selecting team members at the values level creates opportunity to shape the individual for changing strategies. Consider this. Over time, our mission and vision remain the same but, reasonably, the strategy may change. Strategic change at some level is probable as the culture around us changes, as the ministry dynamics flex, and as senior leaders develop, retire, or transition in other ways. We make a mistake, especially in hiring, when we recruit only to a strategy. Maybe you create a new role for the position of family pastor and your church has already taken steps toward implementing a milestones strategy to connect church and home for discipleship. You might make the mistake of favoring only candidates who are currently working milestones strategies in their present areas of service. Instead, assess each candidate's values because the strategic plan called "milestones" will likely give way to a more creative, pragmatic design at some point. A family pastor whose values align with those of the church he serves will be able to think through potential strategies to further the mission and vision and change because he is driven by a value like "gospel transformation." If he is married to a strategy, he will become antiquated in his leadership as the plan becomes antiquated. Hiring at the values level offers long term strategic flexibility in the proper direction. At every level, the best staffing, volunteer or paid, begins at the values level.

Tap to vision. Clarifying your vision allows you and others in your organization to engage potential leaders compellingly by "shoulder tapping" them to vision from the beginning. I would define a "shoulder tap" as an intentional but informal recruiting conversation. The vision of our church is to "Saturate the 4B[4] area with the gospel by restoring people, families, and churches."

Have you ever been asked to serve in a second grade Sunday School class on Sunday mornings? Poorly done, it can go a little like this. "Hey John! Sorry to stop you in the hallway like this. I know you are trying to get to lunch but I need two more people to work with second graders every Sunday morning to have a full roster beginning in August. All you have to do is show up ten minutes early every week, read the lesson, and give them a snack. Can I count on you? I'm sure our Lord would be pleased with your effort to keep kids out of Hell." You know it happens like this often if you have been around church very long. In our desperation, we become great at applying quick, unexpected pressure mixed with some favor of the Lord and guilt to get our recruiting job finished. This rarely works.

Tapping to vision involves potential leaders in the greater purposes of God. Let's take the same second grade Sunday School class and our fictitious recruit, John, one more time. Send a message to John ahead of time and ask him to meet you outside the second-grade classroom on Sunday just after the class begins. Tell him you just need five minutes. When he arrives, thank him for coming. Ask him to look inside the window at the teacher and second graders as they engage the Bible in age appropriate, creative ways. Ask, "John, what do you think is happening in there this morning?" He will make observations like, "that kid is throwing goldfish," or "the teacher seems to be doing a great job teaching a Bible story." "That's all true" you might say, "but John, consider this. Every second grader in that room is part of a home right here in the 4B area. When they leave this classroom after an hour together they will leave with a truth in their mind about the gospel of Jesus Christ. They will take that truth home to families all over our region. Some of their parents are "all in" and will lead faith conversations around their tables today with the guide we hand them as their child leaves the classroom. Some of these children will go home to parents who are spiritually AWOL, carrying gospel truths into families needing gospel transformation. These children are the present and future of the church in our region. Their families are worth our investment. John, I've noticed you seem really great with children. At some point in the near future, I'd like to discuss your involvement in our children's ministry. For now, just pray about making an investment in the next generation as we work together to saturate our region with the gospel."

A planned conversation recruiting to vision is more effective than a "Hail Mary" begging someone to fill a slot. Shoulder tapping to vision invites a potential leader to be part of helping us get where we are going as directed by God. Recruiting people who share values and are compelled by the vision ensures greater buy-in and practical long-term success. Everyone wants to be part of something that is greater than themselves. Even senior leaders want to be tapped to vision in the hiring process. I want to know that what you are asking me to do is worth the investment of my life. Don't hire or recruit people for a job. Ask them to invest their life in the vision.

Necessary endings. Recalibrating for discipleship that engages the family will mean as new things begin, some things will have to end or we will find ourselves stuck. Some programs, once just right, will find a necessary ending. Volunteer leaders and paid staff who navigate the *SHIFT* will either adapt and continue to bear fruit or find themselves in a place of necessary ending.

There are many variables leading to necessary endings. Maybe we have great people in the wrong role and their service in that position needs to change either by ending completely or by transitioning to a different role in the organization. Mistakes are possible as we recruit, requiring leaders to own putting a good person in the wrong position. We need to own that and lead. Perhaps we have a good person on the team whose values do not align but in fact compete, causing constant friction. It could mean it's time for an ending. Some people can become toxic over time, wounding others or jeopardizing the mission and vision. Toxicity, if not corrected, requires an ending sooner rather than later. Maybe a person is half-hearted, apathetic, or lazy in their service. It may be time for an ending. There are many causes for and types of necessary endings, but in each case the ending is necessary for the overall health and trajectory of the team toward mission and vision.

How do you know you have the need for a necessary ending on your paid or volunteer staff? If you are a leader, you know it in your gut. This person keeps you awake at night from time to time. You feel stuck because of this person. Other people besides you are frustrated, stuck, or wounded because of this person. It always seems this staff member is pulling in a different direction causing sideways energy. Practically, this person never does what you ask them to do. You feel burdened by the very presence of this team member. How do you know? You already do.

As you recalibrate, establish a "no egg shells" policy and a process for consistent and fair evaluation. First, squelch team dysfunction by refusing to walk on egg shells around people. Communicate expectations and insist on alignment. Church leaders notoriously avoid difficult conversations with people, bringing harm to even more people and limiting the fruit of the ministry. Second, develop a plan for evaluation at every level that is consistent and fair. Practice the principle of coaching up or coaching out. When we have a problem with a staff member or volunteer, it is right to go to them, highlighting the problem and clarifying the expectations. Real conversation is the first step to becoming better. Potentially, the problem is unknown to the staff member. Shine light on the blind spot. Or, the staff member senses there is a problem as well. Clear conversation will actually bring relief. Develop a plan to help people grow. Take the time to coach them up and if possible continue in the current role. If the issue is skill set but values align, consider them for another role that fits their capability. But, if the person will not coach up, then coach them out. Do not wait too long. Some endings are necessary and recalibration usually reveals personnel issues. Don't be afraid. Pray for wisdom and lead toward a new norm when it comes to staff and volunteer dynamics.

Measuring the New Norm

How do we know the shifts we make involving staff and volunteers are actually causing us to be more successful when it comes to partnering with the family to make disciples? Our temptation will be to measure outputs that seem a bit intangible. Things like unity, story, or fruit become our units of measure. While the output metrics like these seem important they are frustrating to measure. Experiential things are subjective. How do you put a number on unity?

Instead we need to measure inputs or the disciplines and behaviors of our team members related to family ministry. In other words, while it may be difficult to measure "unity" on the team as anything other than a feeling, we can measure the best practice behaviors for a particular role on the team regarding family ministry. Take the senior pastor for example. Clarifying the best practices of the senior pastor in light of the mission, values, vision, and strategy in regard to family ministry, allows us to measure those practices over time. For instance, in the past year did the senior pastor ensure a family devotion tool distributed fifty-two Sundays of the year based on the weekly church experience, to give parents and grandparents a chance to further the conversation at home? We can measure that. Did the senior pastor cast vision for discipleship at home as a major thrust of the church at the state of the church address, in business session and church family gatherings where vision is often cast, and illustratively and doctrinally in sermons? That is measurable.

The same is true for any role in the church. Measuring the input is the best way to measure success. Consider again the volunteer role of a second grade Sunday School teacher. As long as best practices for family ministry are communicated and trained, we can measure the behavior of this team member by asking questions and verifying. Did you clearly present the gospel in an age-appropriate way in the classroom each week? Did you learn the name of the parents, siblings, or caregivers of each child in the class this year? Did you attend all of the equipping sessions for leaders of children and their families? Did you distribute the home conversation tool for families related to the Sunday School lesson each week? Did you personally invite every family represented in your class to Parent Summit this year? All of these things, we can measure. Though the inputs may be different by role within the ministry, behaviors and best practices are both manageable and measurable in every case. To measure successful recalibration regarding the staff and volunteer dynamic, identify and measure best practices for each role.

Summary and Resources

A church focused on making disciples by equipping and ministering to families is only as effective as each member of the team. Simultaneously the team is only as effective as the least aligned staff member or volunteer. While this certainly is not the glamorous part of ministry leadership, creating the right team culture and staff dynamics is key in recalibrating the church for family ministry success. It takes wisdom and courage and the guidance the Holy Spirit. There is no greater cause than Jesus, His Kingdom, and the people, families, and churches that represent our King on the earth. Lead well when it comes to team.

There are three books I suggest reading if this chapter leaves you wanting more. First, *Church Unique* by Will Mancini. It is the best book I have read on creating alignment around mission, values, vision, and strategy. Next, *Necessary Endings* by Dr. Henry Cloud. This will help you know when it is time to lead a person toward a necessary ending and how to do that with compassion. Finally, *The 4 Disciplines of Execution* by Chris McChesney, Sean Covey, and Jim Huling. While this is not a Christian work, it is very helpful for learning to measure inputs as best practices. Recalibrate, friends. It's time.

Endnotes

[1] https://www.jimcollins.com/concepts/first-who-then-what.html.

[2] For assistance on clarifying mission, values, strategy, and vision for your ministry, http://www.willmancini.com/wp-content/uploads/2011/08/Church-Unique-Visual-Summary_Small.pdf or read the book Church Unique: How Missional Leaders Cast Vision and Capture Culture by Will Mancini.

[3] Christian Smith and Melinda Denton, Soul Searching: The Religious and Spiritual Lives of American Teenagers, (Oxford, UK: Oxford University Press, 2005), p. 261.

[4] The 4B area is the geographic region of Southeast Houston and Galveston County from the Beltway to the Beach and from the Bay to Brazoria County.

3
Discipleship: The Four Spheres

Jim Putman

Current Unhealthy Norms

There seems to be a widespread epidemic in the American Church today; an epidemic of young adults leaving the church and even the faith they were raised in, without any desire to return. Many children who grew up going to Bible classes, church camp, and youth group, are now found living a lifestyle far away from the Christian faith and culture they professed to believe in when they were younger. Whether that includes a sexually active lifestyle (heterosexual or homosexual), or addiction to drugs or alcohol, or just a life that no longer prioritizes Jesus and His purposes in any way, it looks far different than what their parents hoped for them.

So what causes this problem? Some parents intentionally and actively did their best to raise their children to love Jesus, only to watch their children choose the world instead. It is true that there are three parts to any equation when it comes to raising children. God's part, the parent's part, and the child's part are all required for a child to take on a relationship with Jesus. A parent cannot do God's part (He always does that), they cannot do the child's part, but the parent can do their own. It is true there are many cases where the parent did their part but the child chose to walk away. It is true that no parent is perfect and always could have done some things differently. Even if a parent could have been perfect, it does not guarantee that a child will choose Jesus. However, the church-world suffers from this epidemic because for the most part it is ignorant or unwilling to do what is required to raise children who know Jesus. The lack of real discipleship in churches has led to a lack of real discipleship at home. This has caused the issues we are now having.

Most adults in our culture grew up in a system that had been built around their parents' work, sports, or even their family. Oh yes many of these people had a weekend church experience intermingled into the system, but very few experienced church as more than a building occasionally attended. Few experienced a family centered around bringing glory to Jesus and serving Him together as its goal. The methods employed in the past few decades didn't work in our American culture. If the same methods are going to be employed in this much more aggressive culture, then the cycle will continue downhill even more radically. In order to break this cycle and change, parents have to completely rebuild around Jesus and His definition of a disciple. Even if they do adopt better definitions and terms (which needs to happen), they will still fail unless they change their methods for transferring their faith on to their kids as well. Sadly most will not do this. Most in our culture are consumer minded and want things easily and quickly. They shy away from things that make them uncomfortable or require faithfulness and stamina. Most have little time because they are focused on many of the same things their parents were focused on as well, but unfortunately to a greater extent. Added to this, they live in an electronic and digital culture that leaves even less time for relationship packed with spiritual truth leading to right belief and action. They are also living in a time when the media has made it clear that it will attack a Bible believing person and family through any means necessary. If our kids go to college, then they are facing an indoctrination center designed to radically change a student's beliefs and values. The old definitions and methods didn't work (for most Christian families) and they won't work now either.

Because the product resulting from our definitions and methods is so lacking, few professing Christians have experienced the life Jesus promised. This leaves those watching on the outside to wonder if what we believe is really true. They wonder why, if what we believe is true, would those who grew up in our churches be leaving? They don't know that Christianity as it was defined and its practices wasn't really Christianity but rather a made-up version co-mingled with the wrong definitions and practices. You see we have allowed the enemy to take our words and redefine them. When we allow the enemy or the culture to redefine biblical words, it may sound like we are talking about the same things. However, the concepts lose their power to change anything. Theoretical concepts and the right information alone does not transform a life. There is a big difference between knowing about something and knowing the person of Jesus. Too often churches have become places of right teaching with little evidence of a relationship showing what the information lived out correctly looks like. So few have the relationships required in the faith that enable us to learn and sustain things that truly change us.

When discipleship isn't lived out within the church because people are too busy, or they don't see that church is far more than a place you go to once in a while, it affects the home in several ways. Parents don't know how to be spiritual fathers and mothers because the best they got growing up was a conversation (maybe) about it. They never actually saw behaviors in everyday life that modeled what those words meant in their own parent's lives. Parents then feel ill-equipped to do the job God gave them to do. At best, they bring their kids to church so the children's minister or youth pastor can teach their kids the stories. Rather than the main disciple makers being the parents, the pastors have become the support, and things are reversed.

When parents don't know how to disciple and have not become mature themselves, any attempt to represent Jesus to their kids can create real problems. Children may learn that it's a nice idea, but they can't really do much in practice. They see a real discrepancy between what their parents say they believe and what the parents practice, or are even able to practice.

When you are born again, you become a spiritual infant and then a child and so on. If most Christians are merely infants or children because many were never parented into the faith, then those who represent Jesus most often in the world are ignorant (not stupid) or spiritual brats. When brats represent Jesus to the world is it any wonder that most don't want to come and be a part of the spiritual nursery? It doesn't look much different than the world they already live in.

Consequently, people attend church rather than becoming part of it. Mainly because there isn't much to be a part of anyway (besides an hour long service)—and if there is, it is painful to get involved because people are hurtful, and there's no real life change. Pastors are gathering crowds and are becoming paid players and the people are becoming fans, who at best become informed spectators but can't play themselves. Rather than a spiritual army that knows how to fight for their families, community, and work places, they are often immature and become victims to the enemy who fights us at every turn. Rather than conquerors, we become victims. When our families experience the pain the world offers and eventually delivers on, there are too few mature disciples able to help. Why? We didn't make disciples who could make disciples.

Many pastors resist changing things because it would be too painful and they probably would lose their job. Most people in their churches are immature and want what they want. They vote with their feet (by leaving) or mouth (by complaining) in ungodly ways. Or they will expel the pastors who will no longer feed in the style desired. They want a church that makes life simple for them.

Families have separated the "church" sphere from the rest of the sphere's in their lives. Not only have they placed it as a separate category, they have relegated it to last place of importance. They have become so immersed in the world that church becomes an optional convenience. Until you return to making disciples who are changed in every sphere of their lives, then parents will not know how to live the part God gave them within their own families.

You can tell what people deem important by the amount of time and money they put toward it. For many families with young children—that would make sports and extracurricular activities very high on the list of values, investing great sums for travel ball and such. Then when practice or game schedules conflict with church activities in their lives, church always loses.

You become a disciple of anything you follow and devote time toward. If your children are watching you put God on the back burner, why would you ever expect *them* to become a disciple of His?

Recalibrate to a New Norm

So where does change begin? How do you ensure raising up disciples who will become fully mature and disciple those around them?

Our church often teaches that God did not send us to make converts—our mission is to make disciples, who make disciples.

Let me start by saying that Jesus had two purposes in coming to earth. First and most importantly, He came to live a sinless human life so He could die on the cross for all who would believe in Him. He came to pay for our sins through His death, burial, and resurrection. Second, He also came to make disciples who would later go and make disciples. These disciples became the bearers of the good news in written form, voice, and lifestyle.

What benefit is it to have good news if no one knows about it? Jesus came to make disciples, but also He came as a model for *how* to do it (live it out so people will want to hear it, know how to share it and teach it so others can do likewise). When Jesus sent His disciples into the world to make disciples, He did not mean "go and do it any way you want." He meant "you have been *with* me and *seen* me make disciples, now go and reproduce the process." **We often say you cannot divorce the person and teachings of Jesus from the methods of Jesus and get the results of Jesus.**

After Jesus died on the cross, He brought His disciples together to give what is commonly known as the great commission. Matthew 28:18-20 says, "… All authority in heaven and on earth has been given to me. Go therefore and make disciples of all nations, baptizing them in the name of the Father and of the Son and of the Holy Spirit, teaching them to observe [obey] all that I have commanded you. And behold, I am with you always, to the end of the age" (ESV).

Very few have been discipled, though they may have heard a watered down version of the Gospel and even been baptized. Very few see themselves as disciples, who are commanded to make disciples. Instead, they call themselves Christians, as if there's difference. Many have taught a Gospel devoid of discipleship. If being taught to obey is just a nice idea, and the Gospel is just hell insurance, then why should they learn to obey? Many, who do preach the Gospel, see baptism as a finish line rather than as a starting point in the process of spiritual parenting and submission; a process leading to maturity. These often well-intentioned evangelists celebrate how many raised their hands and prayed the prayer, but not how many took a step toward real discipleship that teaches them to know the ways of God in every aspect of their lives. Leaders find it easier to measure how many made a "decision" than to know how many lives were truly changed into mature disciples, who make disciples themselves. The effects of this failure are everywhere. Some realize the difference between conversion and discipleship, but often do not clearly define what a mature disciple is.

In church, we talk about maturity as defined in Jesus' invitation to follow Him in Matthew 4:19. The invitation *IS* the very definition of discipleship. In Matthew 4:19, Jesus said, "Follow me, and I will make you fishers of men" (ESV). A disciple of Jesus follows Jesus. He is Lord and a disciple follows. You submit to His leadership and perspective—Jesus then says "I will make you…" this speaks of change. Jesus takes us as we are, but makes us into someone who looks like Him. Romans 8:29 says we are being conformed into Christ's likeness. Jesus is the living Word and He made the point that all Scripture hangs on two commands—Love the Lord with all your heart, mind, and strength, and love your neighbor as yourself (Matthew 22:37-40). So we are following Jesus and He is changing us at our core to love God and others. Finally, He says He will make us fishers of men–disciple makers. Because of our love for God and others, and because we understand the brokenness of the world and God's desire to reconcile not only us but others through us, we join Him in His mission, rather than demand He join us in ours. This changes how we live and what we live for.

A disciple of Jesus lives out this change wherever you go in life. Discipleship can be explained in terms of **the four spheres** (clearly communicated in the book of Ephesians). In the letter to the Ephesian church, Paul starts with the explanation of the **first sphere**—the Gospel and what it means to each of them. He points out to them they had once been objects of God's wrath, but now through faith, they have access to God's grace through faith. Paul further states they were once separate from God's people, but now they are a part through faith. There is one spiritual nation now—Jews and Gentiles.

They are now not only part of the Kingdom of God (a Holy nation) but are also part of the family of God. Their identity now rests in Christ as sons and daughters of God. Paul points out that they have a relationship with God and this relationship fuels them—guides them. Then in Ephesians 2:8-10, he reminds them they have been saved by grace through faith, for good works, which God had planned for them to do. Paul uses the term "body of Christ" in Ephesians, and states that the body has been created in Christ Jesus for good works as a part of the body of Christ. Christ's body, the church, has a mission.

This leads to the **second sphere**—the church. Because of who we are in Christ (He is the cornerstone of the church but also the cornerstone of our lives), we now do what He leads us to do in His church—it's His idea for the building of His church (Matthew 16:18). Paul in Ephesians 2:11 through Ephesians chapter 4, points to the family of God, the body of Christ—His church. We see that the church is a living temple built on the foundation of the Apostles with Christ as its cornerstone. The church is the manifold wisdom of God. We teach that as a disciple of Jesus we are saved to be a part of the spiritual family of believers who live together in relationship and work together in the mission we have been given to make disciples. Paul reveals that the church has leaders who pastor and teach, so each person within it is equipped to serve the body as a whole, in the name of Christ for His mission. Paul reveals what a spiritual family acts like as well. They love one another, forgive one another, encourage one another, etc.

As Paul moves to Ephesians chapters 5 and 6, he reveals **the third sphere** of our lives—the physical family. He starts this section with Ephesians 5:21, which says "submitting to one another out of reverence for Christ" (ESV). As a disciple of Jesus, and because of who He is as Lord and Savior, we obey Him within our human family. Everything we do in this life as believers is because of what Jesus has done for us. Romans 12:1 says "by the mercies of God, to present your bodies as a living sacrifice" (ESV). Jesus says that if we remain in Him we will bear fruit in our lives. In this sphere of our lives, Paul answers the question, "what does a husband, wife, and child within a human family look like?" He gives us guidelines for what every part of a human family looks like.

Some have wondered why Paul started with the church rather than the family. They say, "Shouldn't the home take precedence over the church?" Here's my answer to this: Jesus made it clear that many would lose their human families if they decided to follow Him (Matthew 10:34-37). In that context, the church would be the only family that many of them would be left with. Jesus knows that He created us with the real need for human relationships and the church would fill that need. He also knew that a human family controlled by the world's definitions and behaviors would not fulfill that human need. So, even if you don't lose your family altogether, a human family by the world's design would leave us lacking and wounded. God's family not only becomes a family to the lonely, but a model of what spiritual fatherhood looks like so these new disciples of Jesus could see it, experience it, and then start a new thing in their families. Within the family of God, we learn what relationship requires and what it can look like if Jesus is your Lord and the Holy Spirit is working within you. Paul revealed what forgiveness looks like, what encouragement looks like, and what grace applied in life means.

Real discipleship isn't just about teaching new things, but about giving people a model to look at and coaches to guide them so they can repeat it and this happens within Gods spiritual family. It's not that God is prioritizing the church over the home, but that God wanted to start something new in the home through the model given in and through discipleship in the church.

Finally, Paul moves into the **fourth sphere**, which is the work sphere of a disciple's life. Paul in Ephesians 6 writes about slaves and masters. He was not affirming slavery as a positive thing, but rather acknowledging it existed in that time. When we hear the term "slavery," we relate it to our understanding of American history. Much of the population of the Roman Empire would have been considered slaves at that time. This kind of slavery would have looked more like what we would term employees and employers. Paul again connects what we do in our work sphere with who Jesus is, and who we are in Him. Because we are slaves of Christ, we do what we do in our positions as employee or employer, as Christ would have us do things. In this life, we do what we do because of who Jesus is and what He has done for us. We recognize that in this life we may not be rewarded by those we work for or lead, but if we obey Jesus, at the very least, He will reward us in eternity.

Here is the point of **the four spheres**—I contend that most people have not been truly discipled as modeled by Jesus, and as repeated by the early church in the first century. The result is that most people calling themselves Christians do not understand they are disciples who are called on to grow to maturity in every sphere of their lives. Most know more about what was handed down to them by undiscipled Christians (parents, businessmen, and church members) than by what the Word of God actually says about how to live their lives.

When we don't disciple people according to God's design and in obedience to His Word, they will never experience all God has for them. The early church knew this and they made disciples rather than converts. Acts 2:42-47 tells us what Jesus meant by discipleship happening within the church. In this passage, you see the disciples of

Jesus not only preaching and baptizing 3000 people, but then they organize the church in such a way that the people could be taught in relationship. The people gathered in the temple courts (large group) and from house to house (small group). The people were devoted to the Apostles teaching, which included fellowship. *Koinonia* here means deep-level intimate relationship rather than surface meetings where no one really knew each other.

Earlier in this piece, I wrote that Jesus gave the invitation to follow Him to the disciples. "Follow me, and I will make you fishers of men" (ESV). Imbedded within this phrase is a methodology for discipleship. Jesus was not only saying come and follow me, which speaks of Lordship, but He was saying come *be* with me. Real discipleship must include relationship where real teaching can happen. Real teaching includes questions and answers, accountability, transparency, and modeling. Jesus taught in large crowds and there is definitely a place for this as real discipleship has many aspects to it. But from Jesus' perspective, real discipleship cannot exist if it doesn't include real relationship.

In the book of Acts, the disciples repeated what Jesus had done with them. The disciples taught and the people were devoted to the Apostles teaching, which meant they obeyed them and did what they were told to do. The rest of the results in this passage reveal what was taught by the Apostles. They taught them to meet in relationship often (in fact daily, either in the temple courts or house-to-house). The people not only shared meals, but took the Lord's supper together, which was designed to remind them what Jesus had done and that though they were different, in many ways they had the most important thing in common—Jesus. They prayed together and gave their possessions to those who had need. Why did the first church do this? Because the disciples/Apostles of Jesus taught them to obey all that was commanded by Jesus. This changed the thinking of the

Jewish people and eventually the rest of the Christian world, which included Gentiles from everywhere. These people learned to value Jesus over the world. They learned to value people over their things. They learned to love those who had diseases rather than judge them as those who had somehow gotten what they deserved. They learned what family was really supposed to be, as they heard the teachings of Jesus concerning tax collectors and prodigals. Jesus taught the disciples about God's design for marriage (the Pharisees thought that marriage could be dissolved for any reason). Jesus taught people that the community of believers was built on love and humility, and as you read through Acts 2, you'll notice that an interesting phrase ends the section. It says that the early Christians enjoyed "favor with all the people" Acts 2:47 (ESV). I suspect this means the believers and also the unbelievers. The Scripture says the Lord added to their number daily those who were being saved. Why? Because it's hard to hate someone who is willing to sell their belongings so you can eat. When you see people experiencing what you know your heart longs for, you want in. When there is real community and you are experiencing the Holy Spirit—love—different from what you see in the world, you wonder what is going on. When your children are experiencing true Christianity rather than a muted or ineffectual form, you want in, not out.

The church is where it starts if we are going to get to the family in our culture, just as it was the answer in Ephesus. Pastors are the key; their job, as Paul says, is to equip the saints for works of service in the home, the world, etc. When we pastors reclaim our job definition from the enemy, then some within our churches will accept the mission God gave them. The pastors, churches, and parents who reclaim their roles will lead communities who are different from the norm and will experience the life Christ provides.

This will lead to people having a curiosity about what is going on in there (as the Acts 2 church experienced). This will lead to children being raised in homes connected to churches where real relationship exists. Relationships are like ropes that hold us fast in the storm. Envision places where sermons are discussed and embraced in and through relationships. Real questions will be asked and answered. When (not if) people struggle with their faith, there will be a place to share it and bring it into the light and support will be given. Honesty and transparency will be the norm (because that is real Christianity)— *Koinonia* will be experienced—real deep relationship! We will have the kind of relationship with one another where accountability will be given and received because there has been real relationship and support over years, rather than just a judgment pronounced by an unfamiliar someone. I believe that rightly defining maturity and using a method that can produce it, will again lead to the church storming the gates of hell and prevailing rather than just experiencing a slow fade in the culture.

Measuring the New Norm

When real discipleship is taking place in the home, the lives of the people in it will begin to reflect a change. Their schedule will begin to revolve around church services and events rather than being dictated by other activities. As families begin to pursue discipleship in the truest meaning of the term, there are some measurable changes you can expect to observe in your ministry and in the church:

- **More people visiting:** As a family's inward changes begin to cause outward changes to their priorities and schedule, the people around them will notice, be curious, and want to know more.

51

When families begin to make God a priority in their lives, they will also begin to plan their schedule around weekend services, youth group, church events, etc. Both the parents and the children will begin to talk about and invite others to things that are going on at church, events, or classes that are coming up. You will find you need to bring in a few more chairs for weekend service. You will find people are lingering longer after services to talk in the lobby and get to know each other.

- **More people connecting:** More people will want to participate in church activities that go beyond weekend services.

As disciples begin to follow Jesus and be changed by Him, they will find they hunger for more: more teaching, more community, more involvement. Your ministries that happen outside of the weekend service will begin to grow. You will need to form more small groups, you will need a larger space for youth group, you will have more participation in community events.

- **More ministry growth:** As numbers and relationships grow, struggles and needs will require more ministry.

As new people are entering into a place where real discipleship is happening, they should find that the transparency level among mature disciples is high. They will feel safe to share their struggles and concerns with the groups and friends they are involved with in the church community. And this will lead the church to look for methods to minister to them in ways that can teach and help them in their transformation. From finance classes to recovery and restoration groups, the church body will need to address the needs of the people.

- **More leaders arising:** You will see regular people stepping up to lead when they see a need.

As a disciple is being changed by Jesus, he will want to help others see Jesus the way he does. You will see people stepping into leadership who are not looking for position or authority, but have a humble heart to serve wherever there is a need. They may not feel qualified, but they will feel compelled.

More generational impact: As a culture of discipleship is created and nurtured, you will begin to see multiple generations of disciples.

When mature disciples are made, and they go on to make disciple-making disciples, the results are exponential! Over the course of years, you will begin to see parents, children, and grandchildren who have all been discipled. And when these discipled children grow up and move to different communities, they will continue making disciples. This spreads beyond the walls of the church to the community, the nation, and eventually the world.

When you change the culture of your family, ministry, and church to a disciple-making culture—it can eventually change the world. Which was God's plan from the beginning.

Resources to Explore Further

Real Life Discipleship by Jim Putman
Hope for the Prodigal by Jim Putman
The Power of Together by Jim Putman
Dedicated by Bobby Harrington, Chad Harrington, and Jason Houser

4
The Art and Influence of
Meaningful Conversations

Ron Hunter Jr.

Most may find it easier to restructure a church program or realign the staff than to have a meaningful conversation with their 16-year-old. A typical family drive with our teenagers revealed we were each in our own world. Our daughter, with earbuds, would listen to the latest pop culture music; her older brother enjoyed his playlist in the same style, with earbuds. My wife and I, in the front seat, played our favorite contemporary Christian station, but I'm not totally sure, because I was lost in thought about work. All of us within a six-foot square sharing the interior space of our car and nothing more. I am fairly certain our commute was sadly typical. Families share space more than conversations.

Frankly, if you don't teach parents the art of meaningful conversations, all the other chapters in this book will be an uphill battle. You cannot disciple anyone without a relationship, and relationship cannot occur without meaningful conversation. There is an art to conversation. Not knowing how to have a substantive dialogue feeds the disconnections with those around you who matter most.

While traveling and speaking at a D6 Conference in Asia, I often found myself around people who spoke no English. Likewise, I did not speak Korean. We smiled at each other, nodded, and checked messages on our phones knowing we had stuff in common but could do nothing about it. Today's families lack no language barriers but still occupy the same awkward unconnected shared spaces.

Walking into most churches can feel a lot like that car ride or shared space in another country. People of various ages (seniors, adults, teens, and children) are sharing only casual greetings. The older adults do not know how to connect with church teens because they struggle to connect with their own grandchildren. When asked, older adults might say their teenage grandkids speak another language, which leaves them feeling left alone. Inversely, the teens need to know how to talk to the widow lady who feels that loneliness. The church faces the same set of current norms revealing disconnected families and generations.

Current Unhealthy Norms

As I write this chapter, you may find one detail super interesting: I am an introvert. That detail surprises many because I speak to thousands each year from main stages, in classrooms, boardrooms, and one-on-one. However, conversation does not come naturally for me. I work hard at it. So don't rule out this chapter if talking to others (especially your teenager) scares you. For those of you who might be introverts (or extroverts) and who have not seriously engaged your kids conversationally at a deeper level, there's still hope. The really good news is that your teen desires this connection even though it may start with rolling his or her eyes or deep sighs.

Like me, the introverts in your church don't know what to say, or how to start, or maintain meaningful conversations. The Myers-Briggs[1] data shows that just over half the total people assessed are extroverts (53.8%) and just under half (46.2%) are introverts. That means nearly half your church struggles on a daily basis with routine conversations. Listen up, introverts. While extroverts never meet a stranger, they often feel frustration as they struggle to talk to their own teenagers or young adult kids. This chapter can help.

Parents of preschoolers communicate often with their kiddos as those tiny humans learn to talk and gain vocabulary. As elementary age kicks in and curiosity continues to flow, conversations easily continue. But, around middle or high school, it's like someone replaced your kid with a total stranger. Conversations feel forced; you strain for topics and find it easier to give correction, a lecture, or maybe just relish the silence. There are numerous barriers (not all necessarily bad) that assist in the disconnect, such as television, phones, gaming systems, sports, work overflow, music, and your kids being at other friends' homes. While the next section—new norms for meaningful conversation—sets the stage for answers, a few solutions are provided in this section. Most parents agree that technology is the leading barrier between them and their kids preventing quality conversations.

Barriers to Sharing Conversation

TV. Home living spaces tend to revolve around the placement of the television. That rectangle on the wall symbolically appears placed like an item of idolatry where all can face it, be silent, and learn from it. Maybe that sounds extreme, but consider how much connectional time is stolen from families every night. The most valuable button on your remote is *pause* or *record* allowing you to come back later after shared conversations. When you have the ability to play a show anytime, your kids will notice your choosing them.

Phones/tablets. Phones offer the most unrecognizable barrier because the device provides connectedness but not from the relationships closest to you—your family. You can all sit in the same room but be in separate worlds on your phones. It's really hard to get a teen to connect when they see dad and mom lost in their computer, phone, or tablet. You must become more self-aware by allowing your kids to call foul on you as you do with them.

Gaming systems. One of the biggest parental complaints is how much time is spent on various gaming systems. Ask if you can watch or if your son will teach you to play. Most of all, place limits on what takes family members away into isolated activities from each other, including work from the office. Invite your son into planned family activities. Read chapter 14 of this book (by Turansky & Miller) for more insight.

Sports. Frantic families spend so much time shuttling kids to practices and games. Car time offers more opportunities for isolation with earbuds, ignoring the kids, or simply letting everyone get absorbed into their own worlds. Alternatively, you could implement a rule of no electronic devices or books if the car ride is less than 15 minutes. The commute creates captive space for real connections on deeper topics.

Work overflow. Smart phones have blurred the line between work and home. Plan your take-home work for times not shared with family. Maybe do your work while the kids do homework. Sharing such tasks at the dinner table can also connect you in unexpected ways. Save the work for after family time or bedtime. Intentionally plan for connected time with your spouse and kids each evening.

Music. Music inspires, creates mood, and provides entertainment. It can also create subcultures in the family the same way it does in the church. Each generation enjoys different styles and are often unwilling to share the other's tastes. It is hard to believe that music could so separate people. To counteract the division, make a rule that no music is played for the first 15 minutes of car rides so you can talk. Rotate who gets to play the songs aloud in the car, around the house, and during activities like studying, scrapbooking, reading, cleaning, or favorite hobbies.

Friend's house. If your kids are always going to friends' homes, you get little monitoring or connection. When I was a teen, my best friend had the newest gaming system with all the best games. As you can imagine, the kids hung out at his house a lot. My wife and I decided to budget and make our house the place other kids would want to come. As a result, we got to know our kids' friends and observed how they influenced our kids and vice-versa. Create open inviting spaces like family or bonus rooms and include a gaming system, TV, board games, puzzles, access to good snacks, and speakers to play music out loud.

Sometimes you cannot compete with a friend whose parents are in a different income bracket. It's not always about the gadgets; it's about the love. Making cookies, stocking snacks, and talking to the friends requires little budget but captures the hearts of your kids' friends. Through these steps, my wife became the second mom to many of our kids' friends.

Recalibrate to a New Norm

Conversation provides an excavation tool for relationships. Talking, asking questions, and sharing allows for archeological finds of a relational nature. However, many families never scratch the surface of conversations finding little value in the discovery about each other. Real archeological digs have turned up King Tutankhamun of Egypt, the Rosetta Stone, and the First Emperor of China, which all have been estimated at untold millions. For those who know how to mine those relationships, digging deeper into conversations with people closest to us will unearth treasured connections and a healthy intimacy that will become priceless when facing decisions, temptation, and challenges. You can discover within Scripture many treasured verses on the weight of conversations and words.

Scripture describes the tongue with colorful imagery containing both constructive and destructive power. James 3:1-2 depicts the influence of speech like a ship's rudder, the bridle of a horse, and a massive wildfire burning out of control. But James also emphasizes the refreshing and nurturing aspect of words that build up people.

When parents get into a verbal debate with their teen, parents should take to heart Proverbs 15:1-2 and de-escalate the argument by softening the volume, speaking gently, choosing words thoughtfully, and a utilizing an appropriate tone of voice. When your anger gets riled, Proverbs 17:27-28 reminds you to restrain your negative words; fewer words avoid needless rants that wear a child down. Paul likewise offers sage advice when suggesting that your conversation should be full of grace and yet seasoned with salt (pleasant tasting) in Colossians 4:6, and should build up others (including your kids) in Ephesians 4:29. Parents desperately need to model discipline by showing how to have healthy disagreeable conversations with kids.

God the Father and Christ used conversation to teach, correct, and coach humanity (the kids). God visited the garden daily and talked with Adam and Eve. Post fall, as that conversation changed from physical interaction to prompting, discernment, and prayerful dialogue, you see it modeled in the walk between God and Enoch. Elijah's circumstances allowed him to hear God in that "still small voice." Today humanity interacts with God through Scripture, prayer, and observing His creation. Just as the Heavenly Father desires conversation with His kids, you should desire conversation with your kids.

Regardless of whether you are an introvert or extrovert, it's already been noted that parents struggle with regular, substantive, deeper conversations with their teenagers. The following formula will help you connect in a healthy and fun way. Because you want substance, persuasion, and compassion, remember one of the greatest presidents of all time, Abraham Lincoln. The formula is taken from an acronym—TALK ABE. If you can remember TALK ABE, then you can connect with your teenager or young adult child regardless of their walk with Christ. The TALK conversation formula deepens relationships, and within that level of conversation you be will able to share Christ.

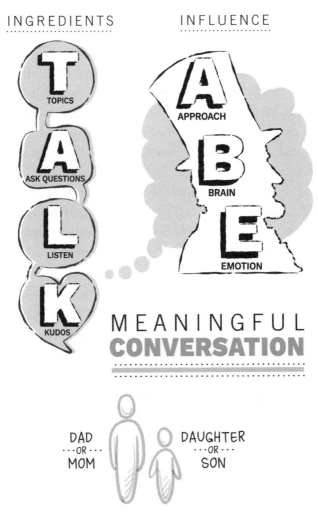

TALK ABE creates a formula for conversation that combines the ingredients of TALK with the influence of ABE. TALK ABE, as depicted on the previous page, shows conversation with TALK bubbles above the daughter and dad, but note the thought bubble ABE flows into TALK, the actual conversation. In short, a great TALK contains Topics, Asking questions, Listening, and Kudos. ABE, the influence part, resembles the 16th president, who could influence people by tackling the most difficult subjects. The ABE acronym stands for Approach, Brain, and Emotion. Look first at the ingredients of TALK.

T—Topics. Selecting the topic creates the entry point for great conversations. At times, the topic comes naturally but discussing the weather or the proverbial "how are you?" greeting creates a frustrating cul-de-sac of a conversation. Find topics that will actually take you somewhere by using these simple topic generators to start a conversation with your kids. Try the *high-low* or *best-worst* approach, which starts like this, "What was the high point (best part) of your day?" Follow up with the second part, "What was the low point (worst part) of your day?" An alternative set of questions helps parents explore the ABE influence portion of the formula, which is to ask about three emotions of the day: mad, sad, and glad. What made you mad today? Sad today? Glad today? These questions lead to deeper questions that progress to value shaping conversations.

A—Asking Questions. Questions allow conversations to be a shared activity. Becoming a good conversationalist is a basic life skill. My wife and I taught our kids the "tennis ball" game. Just as a tennis ball is swatted back and forth on the court, a good conversation tosses questions back and forth. In the beginning, Pam and I actually used a real tennis ball when our kids were around six or seven. Tossing the ball equals asking a question. We would toss the ball to our kids and ask, "What was the best part of your day?" Our daughter or son (whoever caught the ball) would answer and toss the ball back to one of us by asking a question (which at their age was usually the same question repeated back). We would answer and toss back asking about the worst part of the day? Each answer also created a chance to ask "why was that the best/worst?" to keep the exchange going a little deeper. After few times with a real ball, you could announce we are playing the tennis ball game and just toss a question. The mad, sad, glad questions help reveal the values of a child. Our kids learned how to carry a solid conversation because my wife and I learned to ask them questions and taught them how to ask questions in return.

Kids can be the king of one-word answers. How was your day? Fine. What was the best part of your day? Lunch. What was the worst? Math. So you must use some open ended probing questions that nudge them to tell more:

- What made it bad/good?
- Tell me more.
- Tell me about them.
- What do you mean by that?
- Help me understand why that is important.
- What happened just before that?
- What do you think caused that?
- What were others doing?
- What were you thinking during this moment?
- What do you think should have happened?
- What would/should you/they do differently?
- What made that harder than it should have been?
- If you were in charge, what would you have done?

The above questions teach your kids how to think about something rather than just thinking. You are seeking more than information from them by attempting to help them interpret the moments. Such conversations create coachable moments as you can follow-up by helping your kids see what should or could be and what their role is to make that happen.

Part of teaching your children to think is being interested in how they think. Routinely ask for your kids' opinion. Ask their thoughts on work or family decisions you are considering. Then share your thought process and let them get in your head as you teach them to solve problems. My dad, who is super smart in practical ways, asked my opinion one day while I was in college and that was a special moment I will never forget. Your kids do have expertise in areas you have weaknesses: clothing styles, technology, pop culture, and in their studies and hobbies. While you know a lot, don't be a know it all parent—ask for your kids' opinion on stuff.

L—Listening. It should be obvious that conversations are exchanges. You have certainly encountered selfish conversationalists who lack concern about your insight, experience, or opinion. They just vomit words. Don't be the parent who lectures, corrects, or badgers about chores like an insensitive boss or drill sergeant. Teach your kids to listen by teaching them the tennis ball game. Then learn to listen to what they are saying.

My son initiated a conversation during the second semester of his freshman year of college. He was studying at a solid engineering school in our state and wanted to transfer to another engineering program at the university in our city. When he presented his case, he listed the reasons, which included how he needed teachers who cared about his success, practical labs, reduced cost by living at home, and being closer to his girlfriend. Yes, that last reason jumped out, and I focused in on that alone as I began to argue that a girlfriend is no reason to change your university. My son, who is also an introvert, continued to argue that the professors at his current school did not help students who struggled with the more challenging classes because there were many other applicants ready to take their place. But all I heard was "my girlfriend lives in Nashville." He became frustrated because I was not hearing his real issues. During that impasse, I suggested that we sleep on it and revisit the conversation the next day. Beginning to recount the conversation to myself, I realized he made passionate arguments about struggling in a couple of classes and how a new environment may mean the difference of him achieving his career goal or changing his major. I apologized to him the next day. I brought Pam into the discussion. At times, she can see what I am blind to and together we listened, gave our blessing, and helped him transfer. While he and his girlfriend broke up that summer, he went on to graduate as a mechanical engineer. As parents, we need to listen to what they say even when the bigger clues may not be the real clues.

K—Kudos. Do not underestimate the power of affirming your kids. A compliment from a teacher may very well spark a career choice in middle and high school. Key authority figures carry weight with encouragement and accolades. Parents could easily help shape their kids' future by complementing their God-given talents, abilities, passions, and potential. Should not parents help serve as a career counselor rather than some teacher who barely knows your child?

Offering frequent kudos will soften the times you correct your child. However, kids often hear a much higher ratio of correction or judgment from parents than encouraging words. Let them hear 60-80% affirmation of who they are rather than what they have done. In offering affirmation, be very cautious not to create a performance standard by which your kids need good grades, a great at bat, a touchdown, a perfect dance or cheer, or flawless recital to hear your praises. Performance parenting binds kids in a cycle of being dependent on endless approval-seeking actions. When kids cannot or do not meet your approval, they seek affirmation from others often spiraling into unbiblical lifestyles. Providing praise for who your kids are rather than what they do will break those chains, and affirmation melts their hearts. Admire your child's heart in non-performance areas such as compassion, generosity, honesty, ethics, prayer, reading, determination, and other internal characteristics.

Summarizing the ingredients of TALK—Topics, Asking questions, Listening, and Kudos form the ingredients to solid conversations. These skills apply to office talk, dates, and form the nucleus to developing new friendships. If you apply these simple tools, your relationships will deepen because they naturally connect you with the other person. Among the TALK ingredients, look at how ABE creates the influence.

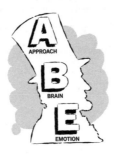

ABE—Approach, Brain, and Emotion form the influential portion of the conversation. Remember, President Abraham Lincoln tackled tough issues and influenced so many when he preserved the nation during the Civil War, issued the Emancipation Proclamation, and delivered the Gettysburg Address. He did not shrink away from difficult conversations or people in the late 19th Century. The men who opposed him and ran against him in the 1860 election—Lincoln appointed them to his cabinet. ABE's approach won over his adversaries into a close collaborative set of advisors. If this connection can happen with politicians, it can happen with your teenagers. Take a look at the ABE. When you see the image above, ABE's top hat shows he is Approaching, the Brain is his head, and the Emotion is the heart issues.

A—Approach. There are two keys to the approach: intentionality and attitude. The first shows you prioritize your relationship with your kids. As a parent, you must approach the situation because your teens will not initiate. They will avoid you through the various barriers listed in the current norm section in order to dodge the previous style of conversations that have been occurring in the home. But using the TALK ABE approach, your kids should resist less and less.

Just like you put others in your calendar and set reminders for events, make sure you position similar priorities for your kids and family. If not, they will get squeezed out. While a congressman, Gerald Ford's ultimate goal was to become Speaker of the House. To get to the top, he refused no assignment or committee appointment. Work took him away from his family every evening, coming home very late every night. Their only daughter who was 10 at the time did not realize she had a father and remembered it seemed odd to have this man join them at the dinner table.[2] Likewise, ministry or careers can create the feeling of orphan-like loneliness for parents with workaholic tendencies. Intentional talk moments are key.

You may be high capacity, fitting more into your day than most but leaving out one key connector: the dinner table. American College of Pediatrics shows the power of family meals around the dinner table helps protect teenagers from negative and high-risk behaviors as they progress through middle school, high school, college and into young adulthood. Research also shows a 30% decline in people gathering around the table for meals.[3] While kids and adults may outwardly desire to eat in the living room around the television, studies also show how most value their time at the table of connecting with conversation even more than vacations or other family activities.[4] The dinner table provides an appointment for structure that kids desire, plus it allows parents to observe the mood, activities, and overall emotional well-being of each family member. In today's socially connected culture, the family meal time teaches kids how to interact face-to-face and get the wisdom of parents in the process. Make the dinner table without TV a routine event more often each week as it will be your conversation incubator.

The second part of the approach shows a most fascinating phenomenon: when you approach your child with a connecting goal rather than a corrective goal, the child will be more receptive. Basically, the outcome is often determined by your attitude when approaching them. My wife and I observed times having a serious corrective talk or discussion with our daughter, and she would get quiet and shut down. We knew to back off rather than push through because the goal was not to get the last word or final directive. We wanted her heart to sincerely desire to obey, not just comply. Your kids can discern your motives—so spend time routinely in normal TALK conversations to deepen your relationship with ABE—approach, brain, and emotion.

B—Brain. Because the brain is not fully developed until around age 25, the choice that makes perfect sense to you as a parent may not make sense to your teenager or even your young adult child. Do not fall into the trap of just telling your child what is right, as their mind will not fully grasp it. They think they know everything, and to some degree they may be right but *their* everything is miniscule compared to the vast experience of everything you have learned. Share more than just the truth with them; share the reasoning that helped you arrive at the conclusion, and teach them how to reason. Your kids must learn to use their brains when facing peer pressure, challenges to their faith, and unhealthy cultural conformity. Just because you are right does not mean your kids will realize it or even agree with it as they are processing through an emotional rather than rational means.

E—Emotion. If your kids do have fully developed minds and do not cognitively see problems the way someone 26 and older does, then what drives their decisions? Because kids have not reached 25, each stage of their little lives so far reveal some level of naivety that fails to grasp reality, like the preschooler's willingness to swap a dime that is smaller for the less valuable but larger nickel, or how the child thinks every "as seen on TV" product works exactly as advertised. Don't think that teenagers have lost all their narrow perspective because they are listening and having most of their conversations with peers.

Because the child learns through relationships, they trust people first and content second. Parents help a child derive most of their early values or judgments about the world along with what is defined as right or wrong. Most of the lessons are caught when the child observes and hears parents, relatives, television, social media, and later from his or her own experiences, good and bad. Kids may trust bad content if they trust the person sharing it, which is why kids grow up as bigots, racists, atheists, and adopt so many other values that a child learns from a parent, professor, or some other respected influencer in their lives.

You can see how kids learn false values through experience and emotion. Kids are shaped from negative emotional experiences like touching a hot stove, being picked last, being told you are bad, feeling left out, guys questioning your manhood, body-shaming your feminine shape, and so many others. The most memorable emotions are often the negative ones, embarrassment, ridicule, pain, or inadequacies. You now see the importance of Kudos from the TALK ingredients to help balance what they feel.

Parents tend to share truth, facts, and what is right, rarely taking time to pull back the curtain on why or how it is right. Combine the truth with emotion by telling stories that illustrate the point. Share personal experiences from your childhood or adult life that helps their minds wrap around the cause and context. Transfer real life examples that paint a picture of why and what rather than just talking in abstract concepts.

Good writing and speaking incorporates the use of emotion, stories, or visuals to reinforce truth. History teaches how emotion serves as the catalyst to unexpectedly change people's thinking. Wilberforce's showing Members of Parliament the slave ships, CBS cameras capturing the Selma Bridge crossing, scratches on the walls of the Auschwitz gas chamber, the American flag raised on the debris of the World Trade Center, watching a presidential candidate sweat in the 1960 election debate, and many other images changed outcomes because emotion affects thinking. Visuals move people because they think in pictures. As parents, remember to use emotional imagery to reinforce values rather than let emotions be the catalyst for values.

Measuring the New Norm

- Bring bright plastic balls to the worship service and teach the parents and kids to play the tennis ball game. Repeat the tennis ball game in church once a month or quarter as it will build relationships and teaches the art of conversation. Then ask families/couples weekly how many days this week the tennis ball game was played.
- Ask parents to share how they coached their kids as result of asking them the mad, sad, glad questions.
- Ask parents who have grown kids away from church how the renewed relationship building is going through the TALK ABE approach. Measure renewed healthier relationships.
- Ask parents to measure the closeness they feel with their teens every month while using the TALK ABE approach (1 being needs lots of work and 10 is could not be better).

- Measure how many seniors can adopt younger kids in the church to use TALK ABE and build prayer support relationships with them.
- A long-term goal is to measure how generations who stay connected reduce the percentage of young people who walk away from their faith and family values.

TALK ABE works as a formula for influence through conversation. You don't need to compete with earbuds or gaming systems if you connect with your child's heart. Fred Rogers, one of televisions most iconic children's figures, worked with a similar formula to launch Mr. Roger's Neighborhood ignoring the fast pace and new animation to just slow down and have a conversation with kids. The purpose of his show was to create a relationship with kids by addressing their curious questions that worried or concerned them. Mr. Rogers knew how to talk to kids even about the most difficult subject matter. You can use the teaching of this chapter to create your conversational neighborhood and talk about what matters to your kids. Use the ingredients and influence of TALK ABE to learn the art of meaningful conversation.

Resources to Explore Further
- *Talking With Your Kids About God: 30 Conversations Every Christian Parent Must Have* by Natasha Craine
- *5 Conversations You Must Have With Your Daughter,* (Revised and Expanded Edition) by Vicki Courtney
- *5 Conversations You Must Have With Your Son* by Vicki Courtney
- *The Tech-Wise Family: Everyday Steps for Putting Technology in Its Proper Place* by Andy Crouch
- *Parenting is Heart Work* by Scott Turansky and Joanne Miller
- *Case for Christ for Kids* by Lee Strobel

- *The 21 Toughest Questions Your Kids Will Ask About Christianity: & How to Answer Them Confidently* by Alex McFarland
- *52 Creative Family Time Experiences* by Timothy Smith
- *The DNA of D6: Building Blocks for Generational Discipleship* (Sand Castles, Snorkels, and Scuba Chapter—helping parents dive deep into conversations) by Ron Hunter Jr.

Endnotes

[1] Paul B. and Katharine D. Myers, *MBTI® Form M Manual Supplement*, (Sunnyvale, CA: The Myers-Briggs Company, 2009).

[2] Scott Kaufman, *Ambition, Pragmatism, and Party: A Political Biography of Gerald Ford,* (University Press of Kansas) pg. 70.

[3] https://www.acpeds.org/the-college-speaks/position-statements/parenting-issues/the-benefits-of-the-family-table.

[4] William J. Doherty, Ph.D., *The Family Dinner Table and the Health of Our Children: Traditional Wisdom and New Data*, (University of Minnesota), http://www.ksre.ksu.edu/humannutrition/DesktopModules/ViewDocument.aspx?DocumentID=8481 accessed February 20, 2014.

RECALIBRATE
Age-Specific
Ministries

5
Fearless Family From Courageous Parenting

Jimmy Myers

Steve and Rhonda were two of the greatest Christian parents I knew. They attended my FamilyLife class at church every week and always contributed to the discussion with wisdom and insight. One evening, after class was over, they approached me with concerned faces and said they needed to talk. I zipped up my backpack and told them I was all ears. Steve began by saying they had great relationships with their kids, including an open dialogue with their two teenagers about a whole host of subjects. Rhonda continued, "Well, Jonathan (their sixteen-year-old) came home from lacrosse practice the other night and asked us which of the two creation stories in Genesis were true. He said a friend who played with him on the team pointed out that in one story man was created first and helped God name all the animals, and in the other story man was created last as God's crowning creation. He said that he didn't realize the Bible was full of such errors and asked us which one was true, and which one was false! Well, there's nothing false in the Bible is there? I didn't even know there were two creation stories...are there two creation stories? We were totally caught off guard and ended up mumbling something about how God works in mysterious ways, and we need to trust..." She looked sheepishly at Steve and said, "I really think we messed that up."

Current Unhealthy Norms

If you are currently working within the church ministry, let me begin with one indisputable fact. Young people, from millennials to generation Z, who have been *actively involved* in their churches, are now leaving the church and abandoning their walk with Christ in alarming numbers. Poll after poll clearly shows that Americans, particularly young Americans, are fleeing the local church in droves. More and more people in this country report they have stopped attending church and have given up practicing their faith in any meaningful way. Among teenagers, about six out of ten will drop out of organized religious activity as soon as they leave home for college or other independent pursuits. A 2017 LifeWay Research study showed that more than 60 percent of evangelical young adults *stopped attending church on a regular basis for at least a year after turning 18.*[1] No matter what angle you approach it from, the results are similar—young believers are leaving the church. This fact is perplexing to pastors, laymen, church leaders, scholars, and parents alike, and there have been numerous attempts to understand the phenomenon and to develop strategies on what the church can do to stem this disturbing tide.

Ever since Jesus ascended into Heaven, God has charged every generation of believers with the task of reaching the society in which they live with the life-changing gospel of Christ. Our task as believers has always been to regenerate ourselves. Our primary calling as parents is to pass the love of Christ along to our children and our children's children. To regenerate our faith through our family. This mandate is made quite clear throughout Scripture. For parents, passing on the heart of their faith to the hearts of their children is now, and has always been, our premiere priority before God.

I know this may sound harsh, but with so many young believers fleeing the Christian faith, our present generation of twenty-first-century parents are apparently being unsuccessful at this task. Parents in America today who call themselves Christians, should find their hearts gripped by the words of Hebrews 12:1: "Therefore, since we are surrounded by such a great cloud of witnesses, let us throw off everything that hinders and the sin that so easily entangles. And let us run with perseverance the race marked out for us" (NIV). Christian parents today are presently losing the race that has been marked out for them. Like never before, there seems to be a disconnect between what parents believe and their ability to communicate and transfer that belief in any tangible way to their children.

You've worked with parents that have sat through so many sermons, Bible studies, and small groups, that if you squeezed them, they'd burp a Proverb, yet they feel totally unprepared to address spiritual issues with their kids. Like Steve and Rhonda in the opening illustration, they are at a loss. Even with all that training, they are petrified that their influence on the child's faith walk will be overwhelmed by secular culture. Their singular focus in their parenting is an astonishing, all-encompassing fear of our present culture, from the internet, to social media, to the aggressively humanistic message of all media and academia. They are afraid this pervasive secular society has become so hostile toward faith, they make most of their parenting choices based on protecting and segregating their kids from the spiritually dangerous influence of the world in which their child lives.

This parental fear is nothing new. Fear-based parenting approach has been around for well over a hundred years. For a people who, throughout Scripture, have been implored to "fear not," Christian parents have most often been nothing short of terrified of the secular culture in which they have found themselves. In the 1920s, they barred their doors to prevent their teenage daughters from becoming "flappers" who wore shorter skirts and listened to—wait for it— Jazz! In the 1950s, Christian parents desperately attempted to keep their young people from viewing Elvis Presley's sexually suggestive gyrating hips—so much so that the Ed Sullivan Show only broadcast him from the waist up in 1956. And don't even mention the Beatles' long hair of the 1960s, living like hippies in the 70s, and who could forget "backward masking" in the 80s. Okay, I can bet some of you are blankly staring at that last one. Google it. Trust me, you won't be disappointed.

The list, of course, could be expanded for each decade. Each generation of Christian parents has felt the strong need to protect and segregate their children from the evils of a godless culture. They're afraid that the coarse language, sexual promiscuity, and the rampant secular humanism that saturates their schools and peer groups will corrupt their souls and harden their spirits. So, they do everything in their power to keep them safely tucked away, segregated from that conflict with culture.

So, let's recap. For decades, Christian parenting has been dominated by an all-powerful fear of the negative influence of secular culture. Because of this fear, they spend all of their time and effort trying to protect and segregate their kids from culture, *and presently* more of our young people are leaving Christianity than ever before in our nation's history. At this point, an old business axiom comes to mind that says, "If we keep doing the same thing, the same way, but expecting a different result, then…we're crazy!"

Parenting out of a fear of culture simply is not working. Never has and never will. It was tried once a long time ago during the monastic era…no wonder it was called the Dark Ages. Fearing the world that God has placed us in is simply ineffective. I'm certainly glad that fear didn't keep young David from his fight with Goliath. The Philistines, you could argue, were the threatening godless culture of his day. Even when some terrified adults did attempt to dissuade him from the conflict, he was undeterred and confronted the giant anyway. And history was forever changed. Instead of keeping our kids out of the cultural fray, we must understand that, just like young David, our kids have giants of their own to vanquish, and their valley of Elah is their local school! God wants to use them here and now, not just when they are grown and out of the house. Constantly protecting our kids is not necessarily honoring to God. In fact, fear is the opposite of faith. How can we stand in the way of God using His children for His purposes? Instead of keeping them locked in our homes, segregated from the giants in the land, let's spend the precious years we have with our kids preparing them to enter the cultural coliseum and win that fight!

Recalibrate to a New Norm

So, if fear is NOT a good focus for our parenting choices, what is? It's a concept we've steadily gotten away from: *preparation.* From the moment a parent looks into their child's angelic eyes for the first time, their goal should be to prepare them. Prepare them to live a life independently dependent on God as their sole source and strength. Prepare them to rely on the presence of the Holy Spirit to sustain them regardless of their life circumstances. And finally, prepare them to exist outside the safe confines of our Christian homes and not to fear culture but to confidently engage it, making an impact for the gospel of Christ in their generation.

And let's be honest. This is not only a failing of the Christian home, it is also a failing of the Christian church. We have done an amazing job of teaching this generation of young believers *what* to believe. Our Sunday School classes, small groups, Bible schools, retreats, camps, and sermons, for the most part, have focused almost solely on salvation and Bible knowledge. And, in many ways rightly so. Kids do need to know what the Bible says as a basis of their belief, to hide His Word in their heart, so they might not sin against Him. We've done such good job teaching what to believe, in fact, that if you asked most any "churched" kid, they would be able to confirm that Zacchaeus was, in fact, a wee little man.

Most young believers are good to go on *what* they are supposed to believe. It is my firm conviction that the process of preparing our kids to confront culture begins by teaching them the *why* of their belief. A new priority must emerge in our discipleship strategies. If we are to help prevent this mass exodus of young people from the church and their faith, my clinical and ministry experience tells me that we must begin vigorously teaching *apologetics*. Early and often. Our kids not only, need to know what they believe, but in today's caustically agnostic world, they must confidently know *why* they believe it.

Now, before you rare back and knock the hermeneutics right out of me, allow me to pause here and assure you that simply teaching kids how to defend their faith and engage in intellectual debate is not and never will be the panacea that will inoculate students from leaving their faith. Only the life changing power of Christ can do that. I recognize that there are factors, too numerous to count, that help contribute to young believers walking away from their belief in Jesus. For example, an exaggerated sense of entitlement, and what Madeline Levine calls, in her excellent, must-read book *The Price of Privilege*, their "undeveloped sense of self." Oh, and we can't leave out another recent Barna Group study[2] (2019) that found that almost half of all Christian Millennials believe that sharing their faith is wrong. Yep, they think it's wrong. So, trust me when I say that I understand there are a plethora of problems leading these students to walk away from their previously held beliefs. Allowing our students to experience the love of their Savior and leading them to embrace the joy of sharing this unimaginable love with their lost friends is THE answer. Yes, our students should be equipped primarily with the love of Christ, however, in today's assertively secular society, like never in my lifetime, equipping them to engage in the intellectual contest of faith is nothing short of a mandate.

Okay, you knew this was coming, 1 Peter 3:15, states, "But sanctify Christ as Lord in your hearts, *always being ready to make a defense* to everyone who asks you to give an account for the hope that is in you, yet with gentleness and reverence" (NASB, emphasis added). Why does Scripture demand this? Because Peter knew that as in his day, there would be our day. A day when the Christian faith would no longer be readily accepted as good news. A day when Christian principles would be scoffed at and ridiculed. In fact, a day when the everlasting Truth of the Holy Word of God would be considered, of all things, *hate* speech. Like in Peter's day, the loving Gospel of Jesus needs defending against a belligerently unbelieving world. I believe that Peter was exhorting believers then and parents and ministers of the Gospel of Christ now, to train up our young people to be ready to give an account for the hope that is within them. To be able to confidently and lovingly respond to the faith challenges from those around them who are, to put it mildly, skeptical about Christianity. That means being able to boldly address questions like:

- How can you say that God is loving, yet be against a woman's right to choose?
- Doesn't evolution prove there is no God?
- Christians seem all about judgment and hate; Jesus was all about grace, love, and acceptance.
- Isn't Christian teaching homophobic, transphobic, misogynistic, etc.
- Don't all faiths basically worship the same god, just in different ways?
- If God is all-powerful and all-loving, how can evil and suffering exist in the world?

You know these types of challenges confront believing kids almost every day. If not in person, then certainly where they spend a majority of their time, interacting online and consuming media. Sadly, we now live in a time that requires you to make sure your students are prepared to address these challenges. Christian students, by the thousands, are graduating from student ministries wholly unprepared for the spiritual and intellectual onslaught that awaits them when they hang up their cap and gowns. The numbers show clearly, they are woefully unequipped to adequately respond to an antagonistically unbelieving culture. The research would suggest that our graduates have literally become lambs being led out to the slaughter.

Let me share one quick story to illustrate why I believe that a basic understanding of apologetics should be standard equipment for the 21st century version of the full armor of God. Dr. Gary Habermas taught one of my doctoral seminars. If you have read *The Case for Christ* by Lee Strobel, you might recognize his name. Strobel interviewed Dr. Habermas for that book because he is the leading authority on the historicity of Christ's resurrection. For decades, he has debated atheistic academic dignitaries from all over the world who apply all their scholarly acumen to convince the academic panel or audience of those debates that the resurrection of Jesus did not factually, historically happen. He has debated numerous renowned atheists and academicians of the highest scholarly order.

In that class, he regaled us with stories from many of those debates, about what his opponents would do, and how he would counter with his own well-reasoned arguments. But one day during a break, I went up to Dr. Habermas and asked, "You've been telling us of all the arguments and debating points that you used when you won debates. But what tactics and arguments did your opponents use against you, when they won the debate?" I'll never forget the puzzled look on his face when he responded, "Well, as far as I know, I never lost."

I, for lack of a better word, was dumbfounded. In all those debates, over all those years, against some of the greatest minds of the past century, Dr. Habermas *never lost* an academically judged debate about whether the resurrection of Jesus Christ historically happened? I couldn't believe it. Can you believe it? Do you think our students would believe that? They need to know when Christians intellectually engage secular culture, even the upper echelons of academia, we don't just do okay, we metaphorically kick butt and take names! We do not have to fear the godless influence of this culture. This culture should fear us—and the impact our well-prepared, reasoned students will have on it.

So, the big question is—how do we do this? How are we supposed to equip Christian kids to be so solid in their faith that the gates of their high school will not prevail against them?

That brings us back to that ever-so-unpopular subject, apologetics. When you mention this arcane word to the average believer, you will typically get one of three answers:

- "What is that?"
- "Boring. Reminds me of 8th grade history class…which I failed."
- "I don't need it. My faith is strong enough without knowing the why."

I know many long for the 1960's American faith experience, when everyone went to church, all stores were closed on Sundays, and school didn't give homework on Wednesday nights so it wouldn't deter church attendance…but we don't. Gone are the days when confronted about their beliefs students can just retort, "The Bible says it, I believe it, and that settles it." In the post-Christian nation we live in today, that doesn't settle it. Not by a longshot. Unfortunately, but realistically, much more is demanded of young believers today, to reach the lost and hold on to their faith.

Our culture contains a paradigm taught in almost every secondary school and college, espoused on virtually all TV shows and movies, and reinforced in the mainstream media that says smart, educated, sophisticated, open-minded, and tolerant people do not believe in God, and it is the rural, uneducated, simplistic, hate mongers who cling to their guns and religion. This covert and overt indoctrination bombards our students on a daily basis. It is crucial that part of our discipleship strategy includes refuting this misconception in the minds of our kids. Why? Because it is factually inaccurate. There are countless examples that thoroughly refute this concept. There are titans of industry, Supreme Court Justices, Nobel laureates, presidents, and world changers in the area of science and medicine who were and are Jesus loving, Bible believing Christians. One quick example that comes to mind is Francis Collins, the head of the Human Genome Project. Our students must be taught consistently, frequently, and over a long duration, that many extremely intelligent and successful people believe in God the Father and His Son Jesus Christ, and when they take a rational stand for their faith in Christ, they are not taking a subordinate intellectual position. Our students must rise up out of their misguided intellectual inferiority complex.

Beginning the process of systematically teaching apologetics is going to be an arduous shift in direction for many churches. To simply add this new directive to an already overloaded student ministry, for example, could cause it to end up as simply another flash in the pan like any other "latest-new-thing." This is going take coordination. And, hey, isn't that what family ministry is all about?! Churches will need a coordinated effort, starting in elementary school, to begin teaching basic apologetics to our kids as one of the key aspects of equipping them to engage with this aggressively secular culture...and win. From womb to tomb, apologetics must become a vital component of our church's overall, long term discipleship strategy.

This is why, I believe, family ministry is the key. Parents are the Willie Wonka's golden ticket in this whole equation. I learned as a psychotherapist who has worked with oppositional, defiant teenagers for decades, that the biggest "bang for my buck" in influencing the behavior of a child, was to equip the parents to change their parenting approach. Once the parents became the central change agent, the child's behavior shifted much quicker and with more permanence than counseling with the child alone. I'm still amazed at how many young ministers don't have Ephesians 4:12 tattooed on their frontal lobes…even taking into account that some may feel that tattoos are a heresy. Our job is to equip the saints to do the work of ministry, not make the work of ministry all about us. We are commanded to equip the *saints* to do it. In this case, we just add one additional "equip." It's our job to equip the parents to equip their kids to give a defense of the hope that is within them, with love.

Measuring the New Norm

As a wise man once said, "Nothing changes until something changes." Truer words were never spoken. Stemming the tide of students leaving the church takes one thing and one thing only. Change. Change in our family discipleship strategies, reexamining priorities, and some rearranging of less successful methodologies. Some relatively simple first steps could include:

- Introducing basic apologetics into adult curriculum, small bites at a time, to avoid overwhelming some folks, is a must.
- Using books like *The Case for Faith* and *The Case for Christ* by Lee Strobel, which for apologetic tomes are easy reads, in small group studies as an instant way of getting the ball rolling.

- Coordinating family and student apologetic curriculum to advocate and encourage discussions at home. Along with promoting family devotionals, also encourage family led faith challenge discussions and the material to do so. When mom and dad are learning and grasping these intellectual discussions along with their kids, the learning that takes place far outweighs a Wednesday night talk from the most impactful speaker.
- Speaking of speaking on Wednesday nights, and Sunday mornings, you need to regularly take on some of the "Hard Faith Questions" from the pulpit. When your kids perceive that these hard questions are seemingly being avoided, they may assume that the critics are right and that the church leadership is afraid to admit they can't actually give those answers.
- Coordinate adult and student retreats and intensives that focus on questions of faith and discuss them and hash them out in fun and original ways.
- Use movies to illustrate challenges to faith that are prevalent in culture and discuss where Hollywood got it wrong. You could do a month of Sundays just on *The DaVinci Code*!
- Make sure that apologetics is included in all evangelism training and utilized during outreach.
- Post hard faith questions on social media and encourage engagement in the spirit of truth with love.
- Make sure your people know that being able to answer all challenges posed is not the point. Not everyone has time to drop what they're doing to obtain a Master's in theological apologetics. One of the most beneficial aspects of your instruction should focus on how and where they can find the answers.
- Therefore, you should stock apologetic books on your campuses and make sure your websites offer links to apologetic

sites online. For example, Sean McDowell has a great article on equip.org entitled *Teaching Apologetics to the Next Generation* that contains tons of ideas.

- Take time to study the doctrines of other religions and cults. Looking at false beliefs is like staring at a counterfeit dollar bill. Look at it long enough and the real thing will jump out at you.

The "getting started" list could go on, but you get the idea. Apologetics must move out of obscurity and into prominence in our worship services, Sunday Schools, small groups, and, most importantly, our homes. And I think you will see your people soon appreciate the effort, as some of their own nagging, unspoken questions/doubts are resolved. Use the previous list to measure how your church is doing on beginning to equip parents on apologetics to equip their kids on the same. We must keep in mind that this renewed effort at preparing our kids to stand against the secular attack on faith is one of the most important priorities to retain future generations of young believers. Preparation will help drain the paralyzing fear that Christian parents face every time their child leaves their home.

I know this is asking a lot from already overworked, and in some cases beleaguered, church staffs. Young Christians families have more than enough to say grace over and need another "priority" like a hole in the head. But the truth is this is our culture. These are the times in which we live, and we have been placed here by an all-knowing, all-loving God for the purpose of impacting this culture with His Gospel, not running from it. Yes, these are unprecedented times to be a Christian in America. Yes, we are facing challenges that our grandparents would not have thought imaginable. Yet, here we are. You've been called to lead His bride in this place and time in history. As daunting as the task may seem, let me leave you with one other indisputable fact: God has raised you up for such a time as this!

Resources to Explore Further

- *The Case for Christ: A Journalist's Personal Investigation of the Evidence for Jesus* by Lee Strobel
- *So the Next Generation Will Know: Preparing Young Christians for a Challenging World* by Sean McDowell and J. Warner Wallace
- *A Practical Guide to Culture: Helping the Next Generation Navigate Today's World* by John Overstreet and Brett Kunkle
- *Surviving Culture: When Character and Your World Collide* by Edward E. Moody
- Surviving Culture: *When Character and Your World Collide* (Parent Edition) by Edward E. Moody

Endnotes

[1] https://www.christianitytoday.com/news/2019/january/church-drop-out-college-young-adults-hiatus-lifeway-survey.html.

[2] https://www.christianitytoday.com/news/2019/february/half-of-millenial-christians-wrong-to-evangelize-barna.html.

6
Grandparenting the Way It Was Meant to Be

Jim Wideman

If you know anything about me, you know I'm a family guy. I love and adore my family. If you know anything at all about my ministry, especially before the Family Ministry Movement, my roots go deep within the early days of the modern Children's Ministry Movement. I wish I could tell you I woke up in church one day and heard the voice of God about a need and an opportunity that was missing in the Body of Christ Universal. But I didn't. I heard the voice of my pastor telling me to grab a guitar and my Bible, go to Children's Church, and don't come out. I had been drafted. You see what caused me to become a champion for families and get involved in helping teach parents to be better parents was becoming a parent. Fast-forward thirty or so years and here I am again seeing firsthand a need that is staring me back in the face as I look in the mirror. The question is, are you and I willing to call for a reformation or recalibration of an institution as old as time that has spun way out of control?

Have you ever found yourself at a place in your life where you knew that life as you currently know it, was about to change forever? I know I've been there; you have too. Imagine yourself standing in back of a church with your oldest daughter by your side. Up to this point, you have only seen one other young woman look so beautiful in a wedding dress (your wife). As you try to decipher and decode your emotions about this first hand collision with ending one season and beginning a new one, you can best describe that sick feeling in your gut as happiness and sadness at the very same time. I know exactly what you are feeling, because I've lived it twice. As a parent, the diaper years seem to be lived in slow motion, for the rest of childhood including the teen years to go by so fast. I've never met a parent about to give away a child in marriage who didn't think it just went by way too fast. Before you take that dreaded first step down the aisle, you stand at the back of the church with your daughter at your side and the only question that is running repeatedly through your mind is, "How did you get here?" It seemed like it all went by so quickly. One day you are going to ballet and piano recitals; you've gone from teaching her how to ride a bike to how to drive a car and now you're walking your little princess down the aisle of a church, then all of a sudden you have a thought, that comes out of nowhere. This is not bad, it's actually a good thing; it's a crucial and necessary step in God's ultimate plan to make you a grandparent. Where did that thought come from? It came from God, the author and inventor of grandparents. The more you think of the possibility of this happening, the more excited you become. Just think, after this ceremony, a brief time of pictures and a little cake the honeymoon begins and you and your spouse are now entering the lottery to have the opportunity to be promoted from parent to grandparent.

Do you remember the day you became a parent? Of course you do! Who can forget that day? Until your child's birth day, every person you have ever met, including your spouse, you had to get to know them for a season, before you realized that you loved them. This was not true with your kids, the minute you laid eyes on them there was a love planted deep within your heart from Father God for each of them that you could not explain. After talking to parents about this big day, most say this was the first time they think they truly understood how much Father God really loves us and desires to have a relationship with us. As you think about how wonderful the day you became a parent was, could you also imagine the love that will explode into your heart and soul when you see and hold your grandkids for the first time? Take it from a guy who's been there twice and wants to go there again, it's amazing!

Current Unhealthy Norm

It's crazy, but after your children get married you seem to be bombarded with questions from friends and family: when are they going to make you a grandparent? The more you think about it the more you find yourself consumed with one burning desire; YOU WANT TO BE A GRANDPARENT! But are you ready to be one? What resources are available to you from the local church? Until I became a grandparent, I never saw the great need and untapped potential of a grandparent ministry. If the church is honest with itself this is a wide-open ministry opportunity. The trouble is grandparents don't know they need help being a grandparent because they don't see God's purpose for grandparents and why should they? Have you ever heard a sermon or teaching on its purpose?

Few have really researched what God's Word says on the subject or looked for a book on the role or function of a grandparent. Has it ever crossed your mind to offer a class on grandparenting, or have you heard of someone looking for a grandparent class to attend? Chances are you may have attended a childbirth class; you may have attended a prep class for parenting. I hope you dedicated your child to the Lord and promised to raise them according to God's Word, but who needs to prepare for becoming a grandparent? Compared to raising your own kids, how hard could this be? What every new prospective grandparent knows from your friends at church is that grandkids are grand and they are just better than your kids! You don't need a class to teach you this. Maybe you've heard, "Grandkids were the reward for not killing the first bunch." That's why I hung in there and never gave up, so I could claim my reward.

As a parent you know firsthand that parenting at every phase of a child's development can be challenging. It also looks completely different as you move from one phase to the next. There are some days in the life of every parent where being a parent looks a whole bunch like work. Somehow when you talk to grandparents who have gone before you, you get the opinion that this time around, it's going to be more fun than it was the first time. After years of observing the role of a grandparent from other grandparents, it seems simple: it's about just having fun. You spoil your grandkids rotten; you buy them whatever they want—especially the things that their parents say no to. That's how you prove to your grandkids you love them, isn't it? It's like you are now a part of this great competition with your own children over who has more influence over their children. Every grandparent knows that part of being a grandparent is that you get to feed your grands whatever you want to feed them or to bake or buy whatever the grandkids are asking for because it's just a known fact that everyone knows, grandparents don't say "no." Even when your kids tell you to make sure the kids take a nap while you are keeping them, you don't have to do what they say for you to do. This is your time with your grandkids. Besides, you're the parent of the parent. What do your kids know about being parents anyway? You're the expert, who do your kids think parented them. You're the trained professional with years of experience. Your kids turned out all right didn't they? The other thing that makes being a grandparent better than being a parent is when you're done or just plain ole tuckered out you just give those hyped up, irritable, and tired little folks back to the parents from which they came and you get to go to bed early, go back to "your life" and let your kids deal with calming them back down from all "the fun times" at grandma's and grandpa's.

Recalibrate to a New Norm

This is not what God had in mind when establishing the role of a grandparent. That's why grandparents need to recalibrate and bring it back in line with God's original design and purpose for the family. Within the Family Ministry movement, you hear a lot about the importance of the church partnering with parents in the spiritual development of their children's faith. If churches should be partnering with families in helping the spiritual formation within a family, what would happen if grandparents would realize it's not about you, it's about partnering with your kids to reach your grandkids and help train them for a lifetime as a Christ follower? What if the church provided "grandfriends" for families within the church that didn't have grandparents but wanted help in passing faith to the next generation? Can you also imagine the possibilities for ministry to happen as families within the church adopted older people who didn't have grandkids? Talk about a win-win for both the families and also those older saints who would be ministered to by a loving family.

I think it's normal for all parents, especially grandparents, to take advantage of 20/20 hindsight in how they want to parent and grandparent differently than past generations. When you became a parent weren't there things you wanted to change about how you were parented? My wife Julie and I came from two very different parenting styles. There were takeaways we appropriated from both and some things we came up with on our own. The thought of becoming a grandparent excited me to think that Jesus was giving us a second chance to shape young lives more effectively in every way now armed with years of experience and a bit more patience. At least for Julie and me, we had somewhat of a clue what a parent should do. Even though you made the rules the first time around, it's very important that you allow your children the freedom to parent differently than you did. Your grands have personal devices that your children never had. The waters you navigated as a parent aren't the same waters today's parents are navigating. Your grands will grow up and work jobs and have careers that didn't even exist 20 years ago. Some of the jobs ahead for our grandchildren haven't even been invented yet. The role of a grandparent is not upper management, but a support team to help your family succeed at carrying out a spiritual legacy to future generations.

Church leaders must equip parents and grandparents to identify the goals of grandparenting as more than just fun, and help them see themselves as a team member who partners with their children to establish the cultivation of faith for future generations of your family.

You know God created the idea of family for a purpose, but what about the role of a grandparent? If you look at what God created without really looking into the purpose or reason it was created, you may start attaching your own purpose to the creation rather than understanding God's purposes.

Let's look at Deuteronomy 4:9, "Only be careful, and watch yourselves closely so that you do not forget the things your eyes have seen or let them fade from your heart as long as you live. Teach them to your children and to their children after them" (NIV). Here is the first time the descriptive role of grandparent is mentioned in the Bible. Not only are we to bring children into the world, but also first and foremost we must teach them to remember and pass on what God has done for us. Each believer has a God story. When I look back and I think about my life and everything God has done for me, I see how He was always looking out for me no matter how stupid I was when I tried to do life my way rather than His way. He always provided for me and placed people in my life to be a difference maker and a blessing to me. I want that fact passed on to my heirs! I love how this Scripture is worded, "Only be careful, and watch yourselves closely so that you do not forget the things your eyes have seen or let them fade from your heart as long as you live." We've all been there, done that and have the T-shirt. Throughout my life and still today, God has done and is doing wonderful things to me and for me. He's done things only He could do. If we're not careful to watch ourselves closely, we forget about all the things we have experienced and are experiencing God doing. This verse goes on to say don't let these things fade from your heart as long as you live. Do you have a journal or book where you keep your family's God story written down so you can remember all the things God has done for you and your family and teach them to your children and grandchildren? What a wonderful legacy to pass on to your family. Maybe it's written in your Bible. My girls know mine and Julie's God stories. We have told them about Jesus' love and grace to us their whole life, how Jesus supplied for our every need, how He has healed us, and how He can and will do the same for them. They have been told of the faithfulness of God over and over again, and now we are proclaiming these things to our grandchildren.

When both my grandsons were born, everyone was at the hospital. We were all sitting in the waiting room, and every time someone came in the waiting room or a phone would ring we would go nuts asking questions. We were all anxiously waiting for news from Cory (my son-in-law) and Yancy (my daughter) on how things were going and if those little guys had shown up yet. Time didn't matter. It didn't matter if we had anything to eat or drink. No one was about to risk for a minute not getting to see and get their hands on those little fellows. Sure enough they showed up into the world and everyone began snapping pictures and trying to get their hands on these new grands and nephews. Those were days I'll never forget. But the next day was a totally different story. Some family members went home, some were ready to see the sights of Nashville, and everyone was up for something tasty to eat. Both times I sat quietly, patiently waiting to see if I could pull off alone time with Yancy and the new baby. The good news I have to report is that both times my plan worked like a charm. The whole bunch left and there we were, just the three of us. Yancy looked at me both times and said the words that I wanted to hear. "Dad, do you mind babysitting and let me go take a shower?" Did I mind? Of course I didn't mind being left alone with my grandsons, which by the way was my plan all along. I remember saying to Yancy both times the same response, "Take as long as you want. You can take a two hour shower if you want; I'll be just fine." Really, I was more than fine, I was in heaven. As soon as the door shut, I began telling those boys the God story of our family. I introduced myself to them and told them we were going to be very close and have a very special friendship. I told them that I would always be there for them and I promised to be an example of a godly man for them to follow. Then I asked them the question I had looked forward to asking them ever since I found out they were coming into the world. I asked them, "Has anybody told you about Jesus?" Since neither one answered me, I just began to tell them about Jesus and what He had done for our family. I told them what Jesus had done for their Daddy and Mommy. I told them about what Jesus had done for their "G & GG." I told them about what Jesus had done for Aunt Woo, and I told them for the first time something I would tell them every day of their life: that God had big plans for them. One of the first Scriptures I told them and wanted to have underlined in their Bibles was Jeremiah 29:11, "'For I know the plans I have for you,' declares the LORD, 'plans to prosper you and not to harm you, plans to give you hope and a future.'" I also told them for the first time something they would hear me say to them for the rest of their lives. "God's plans for you are better than any other plan you could ever come up with, on your own!"

When Rhythm, Yancy's youngest was born, I got to tell him about his big brother Sparrow's God story and how blessed he was to have a godly big brother who would also set an example he could watch. I got to show and talk to Sparrow about the role of a big brother from God's Word. I've continued every day of their life telling them what Jesus is doing and how He's working in our family, and teaching that to them so they can teach it to their kids. I also am quick to point out God's blessings in their lives, in real time as they live it. I tell them over and over what great parents they have and how blessed they are to have such good parents. I reaffirm their parents and work hard to present a unified front, just like I worked hard to present the same to my own kids.

This is why we must recalibrate grandparenting. It's not about you, grandpa and grandma, it's about partnering with your kids to build a spiritual legacy within your grandkids' and great grandkids' lives so they know what God has done and wants to do in their life. Your God story is not just a history lesson; it is still being written today. God is not done with you and your family. Imagine the church coming along side grandparents with ideas and information on how to pass on faith, and where grandparents are learning from each other. Imagine the church providing a place for grandkids, grandparents, and parents to provide passing on special Scriptures, events, and God moments from one generation to another. I hear your question, "What about the kids who don't have grandparents and even the adults who don't have grandkids?" Here's a place for the church to help create "grandfriends" as well as meet real needs for the passing of spiritual heritage from one generation to the next. When I think about the purpose and meaning of each of the Jewish Feast days and celebrations, you can sum them all up with, "Remember what the

Lord has done and teach them to your children." Grandparents and grandfriends can remember what God has done along our past and present journey and teach this to the other generations to pass faith to future generations.

Measure the New Norm

As grandparents and grandfriends, you are the ones who must help transfer the faith legacy of your family from one generation to the next. So, let the recalibration begin. Will you help forge a partnership between parents and grandparents that empowers them to join forces together to start the transferal of faith from one generation to the next?

- Church leaders and ministers must be intentional about making this transferal of faith from one generation to the next a priority and part of the church's mission; not just something we talk about, but something we do intentionally. Does your church begin the generational ministry conversation, using common language to empower grandparents to sit down with their kids and honor them as the parents of their grandkids, submitting to their rules and leadership? Nothing is more confusing to grands as having a different set of rules at different places. Be consistent.
- Rethink your Baby Dedication process to include the role of a grandparent. Does it include a charge to grandparents and extended family and friends and have them make a commitment to be a part of the transferal of faith?
- Do you present a Bible to each family so grandparents and extended family can begin to pass on to each newborn the truth and wisdom of God's Word from each generation to the next?
- Do you provide small groups and/or quarterly events for grandparents to learn from one another and even work on

what needs to be passed down together? Serve? Measure it by Deuteronomy 6 for teachable moments in the home.

- Are you identifying small groups and/or classes to help partner and teach parents, grandparents, even aunts and uncles to partner together to transfer faith from one generation to the next? In addition to your preparing for parenting class, include preparing for grandparents redefining the purpose of passing faith to the next generation.

- Do you provide hands-on instruction to older people about how to use technology? This might be something you have the student or college ministries do to promote multigenerational ministry to take place.

- Do you train older adults to do long-distant grandparenting to pass on faith to their families who live in another location?

Could the success rate of the transferal of a burning, active, intimate faith, from one generation to the next, be significantly greater and give us a totally different outcome with this recalibration of traditional grandparenting? I know it can and I see it working in my own family as I partner with my children to become a better person, have a better marriage, be a better parent, and eventually take my place to pass the spiritual heritage of our family to the next generation.

The possibilities and benefits for grandparenting ministry in the church are endless. What is Jesus stirring in your heart right now, that is missing in your church, to encourage and equip biblical grandparenting and the passing on of faith from one generation to the next?

Resources to Explore Further:

- Legacy Coalition—Grandparenting Ministry www.legacy coalition.com

- *Overcoming Grandparenting Barriers: How to Navigate Painful Problems With Grace and Truth* by Larry Fowler
- *Equipping Grandparents: Helping Your Church Reach and Disciple the Next Generation* by Dr. Josh Mulvihill
- *Biblical Grandparenting: Exploring God's Design, Culture's Messages, and Disciple-Making Methods to Pass Faith to Future Generations* by Dr. Josh Mulvihill
- *Long-Distance Grandparenting: Nurturing the Faith of Your Grandchildren When You Can't Be There in Person* by Wayne Rice
- *Extreme Grandparenting* by Tim Kimmel

7
Young Adults Are Not the Gap Into Adulthood

Jay Strother

Where Are the Young Adults? Look at the demographic makeup of most churches and you'll notice one age group noticeably absent: young adults (ages 19-29). We make much in our D6 churches about reaching "all generations," and yet most churches treat young adults as an afterthought, seeing these years as just a "gap" into adulthood. Due to shifts in our culture and the challenges of life transition, it's easy for young adults to "slip between the cracks" of our churches. Rather than seeing these years as a spiritual "no man's land," ministry leaders need to see that these are crucial years for spiritual formation and shaping the values of a life spent on mission with Jesus.

Pastor and author J.D. Greear illustrates the unique nature of reaching young adults in the early days of his ministry at Summit Church, which is located near several major universities in the Raleigh-Durham region of North Carolina. A few college students stumbled into Summit Church one Sunday, invited their friends, and they soon had a growing contingent of university students. One Sunday morning an usher brought the pastor a peculiar finding in the offering plate: a bacon, egg, and cheese biscuit. Attached to it was a note quoting Acts 3:6: "*Silver and gold I have none, but such as I have, I give to you.*" In addition to getting a good laugh, the leaders of the church took note: "We quickly realized that although this growing number of college students would probably never contribute much to the budget of our church, we would have plenty of potential missionaries."[1] They developed a ministry strategy to enlist graduating college students to start their careers in a strategic city where they could be a part of a church planting team. Over the years hundreds of college students have been mobilized to strengthen church planting projects. Summit Church now celebrates that there are more people worshiping at their church plants than are currently worshiping at their own church. This is a great example of recalibrating ministry to both meet the needs and take advantage of the opportunity of working with young adults.

While not every church is located near thousands of university students, most churches are near high schools who produce this 19-29 demographic. Every church has the opportunity to reach and invest in young adults who are not just the church of tomorrow, but a vital part of the church today. Let's take a closer look at the challenges our young adults face and be encouraged that they resonate with churches who recalibrate their ministries and mission measures to be more biblical, not less.

Current Unhealthy Norms

The first job of a leader is to define reality. If we are going to recalibrate ministry to young adults in our D6 churches, then it's important for us to understand what is happening and to carefully consider why. Most church leaders intuitively know that churches are struggling to reach those in the 19-29 age category, but they haven't put time or effort into reaching this demographic. Within the majority of churches, young adults have very little influence— they aren't in key leadership positions, they aren't represented in important strategy meetings, and they don't give much financially. Therefore, they are easily overlooked, and the assumption is made that they'll "get back in church" when they "settle down," get married, and start having children. The problem with that way of thinking is two-fold. First, it means that young adults are often absent from our faith families during a critical period in their life when they need wise counsel and biblical truth. Second, it's based on dangerous assumptions—that they will *want* to come back after being away and that they'll pursue having a traditional family in the first place. Instead of making assumptions, let's look at the reality our young adults are facing.

Finding your way as a young adult in our culture isn't easy. As ministry leaders, we love to joke about millennials who can curate an Instagram following of thousands, who develop refined tastes for single-origin sourced pour-over coffee and overpriced avocado toast, but who are still living in their parents' basements. Behind our jokes is a reality: transitional phases of our lives are difficult, and it's not an easy time to be an emerging adult. There used to be clear pathways for young adults in life-defining areas of education, career, and relationship. Now it seems there are more options, but also more confusion in all three.

First, higher education has become a complicated and expensive mess. While a four-year bachelor's degree was the standard, intense competition for fewer corporate jobs means that many feel the pressure to get graduate degrees and beyond, adding years of stress and the yoke of student loans. Second, changes in the global economy have dramatically changed the workforce, undermining the number of stable, lifelong careers available. These jobs have been replaced with more fluid career paths marked by low security, more frequent job changes, and the need for new training to keep up with constant shifts in technology.

These changes for young adults emerging into independent adulthood have also had an impact on marriage and family decisions. While half a century ago, most young adults were anxious to marry, find a place to live and start a family, changing social norms have also led to an extended period of single adulthood. The average age of those getting married for the first time has risen from age 21 in the 1950's to age 28 (27 for women, 29 for men) today. When young adults stay single longer with historically unprecedented freedoms, there is a ripple effect of related issues like sexuality, co-habitation, and the development of addictive behaviors.[2] And the jokes about young adults living in their parents' basements? The stereotype is rooted in reality: with cost-of-living increases, parents are more willing to financially support their millennial or Gen Z child into adulthood than ever before. According to best estimates, parents are helping to subsidize their young adults to the tune of almost $40K in assistance between the ages of 18-34.[3]

Fewer young adults are engaged in church. The lack of young adults in our churches can't be disconnected from several streams of trends that are affecting the entire church. First, church attendance is declining as a whole. According to Pew Research Center, the number of adults who identify as Christian fell from 78% to 71% between the years 2007-2014. The much-discussed "Rise of the Nones" (those who identify as "religiously unaffiliated") jumped to 23% of American adults during that same period. While a few conservative denominations are holding steady, no major Christian tradition is growing in the U.S. today.[4]

Next, data supports the visual evidence that our churches are "getting older" as well. U.S. Census data shows that adults aged 19-29 make up 22% of the entire US population. Yet that same age group represents less than 10% of church attendance.[5] Finally, for years there has been a much-debated statistic in ministry circles called the "dropout rate"—how many young adults stop attending church after high school graduation. Multiple studies have addressed this issue in recent years, most agreeing that the range is somewhere between 40-59%.[6] Newer research has been following this trend into the young adult years to see if those who attended church as teenagers do indeed, "come back to church." This research shows that most young adults who attended church as teenagers still believe in God, yet many no longer consider themselves "devout." Two-thirds of those who were active in high school dropped out for at least one year as a young adult. Their time away from the church has led many to question core convictions during a critical time in which they are making life-changing decisions. For example, out of those who dropped out at some point, only 40% say they still "agree with the beliefs taught by my church." Scott McConnell, executive director Lifeway Research sums the findings this way: "During the years most young adults are gone from church, they tend to hang onto their faith but don't make it a priority."[7]

Our methodology has contributed to the young adult gap. While we can point to the societal issues of emerging young adulthood and declining attendance in our churches as cultural contributions to the challenge, we still have to face the reality that our ministry approach to young adults is lacking. First, we need to recognize the reality that many of our young adults grew up in churches that were built around age-segregated ministry models. These models attracted large numbers of young people to our ministries and churches, but didn't create the foundation for a sustainable faith beyond high school graduation. When many young adults graduate from the youth group, they don't know how to find their place in the larger church body. While the D6 and family-equipping movement and other disciple-making movements have been trying to course-correct this issue for well over a decade, there is still much work to be done to wean parents and church leaders from entertainment/attractional models of ministry.

Second, we need to recognize that we have been slow to embrace young adults in all areas of church life including areas of mission and leadership. Worship gatherings and small group Bible studies are important to young adults, but the opportunities in our churches are too often narrow and limited. If all we offer young adults is "sit and learn" opportunities, then young adults who are energetic, passionate, and who feel they have something to contribute will find other outlets in our culture that will allow them to be full participants and not merely sidelined spectators. In an era in which young adults are feeling empowered through technology to develop innovative solutions to some of the world's greatest problems, it's no wonder they are bored by being told to come and sit. Young adults want to contribute creatively to the mission of the church and they are looking for mentors who will develop them into leaders.

Recalibrate to a New Norm

Reaching young adults is not easy because there is no "one size fits all" strategy. Young adult ministry doesn't happen in a vacuum and there is no single program, event, or ministry idea that will make the difference. Instead, churches that are having high impact among young adults are intentional about recalibrating their ministry strategies to include and integrate them into all parts of church life. Just like a D6 church can't simply add programs and events aimed at families to reach them, churches that want to effectively reach and disciple emerging adults must create a culture that considers young adults important and valued. The following are four platforms that mark how churches are recalibrating ministry to include and reach young adults.

Cultivate a disciple-making culture in your church that elevates but doesn't idolize families. As a pastor who embraces a D6 family-equipping model of disciple-making, I hear concerns all the time from ministry leaders that this ministry approach leaves out (or under-serves) singles, senior adults, non-traditional families and yes, young adults. My response to these concerns is that if you think D6 is only for traditional nuclear families, you're not thinking big enough and you misunderstand Deuteronomy 6 (on which D6 is based). In fact, serving in a church context in which we have a significant young adult population, I would argue that reaching young adults is crucial to creating a family-equipping culture in your church.[8] We discovered a long time ago that if you are targeting only parents, you aren't starting soon enough. The value of disciple-making in homes of every shape and size is best developed long before children come along. We want our graduating high school seniors to be equipped to take seriously the call to disciple others in whatever context they find themselves. We teach our college students to lead Bible studies in the common room of their dorm and we equip our young adults to lead Bible reading groups that meet weekly in their apartment. By leading our young adults to practice discipleship outside of church-driven small group programs and events, we are building a habit and practice that disciple-making happens in the home. When they get married and start having children, it's only natural for them to study the Bible, pray, and develop faith in the home because they have been already been doing it their entire adult lives!

In our church and among our young adults, we unashamedly elevate the importance of the family. We teach biblically and honestly about God's design for manhood, womanhood, the role of the home in faith formation, and as a launchpad for lifelong mission. Because so many young adults have a distorted view of the home based on their own life experiences, we deconstruct our culture's distorted values and we reconstruct an understanding of the home through the gospel story—creation, fall, redemption, and hope. In a world determined to redefine marriage and undermine the fundamental importance of the family, we must give young adults the truth about the blessings and challenges of marriage and parenting. But while we believe in the importance of the family as the foundational building block of church and society, we believe it is not ultimate—only Jesus is ultimate.

In some of the most challenging passages in the Gospels, we are reminded that Jesus challenged the prevailing attitudes of His own culture about the traditional family. In Mark 3:20-21 and 31-35, Jesus' own family had become concerned about His ministry practices and had come to "seize him" and take him home. From His family's perspective, Jesus had become a religious fanatic who was hurting the family name and who had become a danger to Himself. In that era, your identity was not centered around the individual but was based on your group status, and the family was the most important group you could belong to. When Jesus is told that "Your mother and brothers are outside," he responded with a shocking statement. "And looking about at those who sat around him, he said, '*Here are my mother and my brothers! Whoever does the will of God, he is my brother and sister and mother*'" (ESV). Jesus was not saying that we should dishonor or neglect our earthly families. But he was making the radical and revolutionary statement that his "true family" is not those who are biologically related to him, but those who have responded to him by faith. This is good news for the scores of young adults who come from broken families or who have no healthy earthly family relationships at all. Our young adults need to know they are fully part of the "family of families" that make up the church. Instead of relegated to "second-class" status in our churches, they need to be invited over for family dinners, integrated into our intergenerational Bible studies, and considered highly for leadership development.

As ministry leaders have noted, one of the acceptable idolatries among evangelical Christians today is the idolatry of the family. While we want to elevate the importance of the family and strengthen the home on every front, we simply cannot elevate traditional family values over the gospel itself. The picture of faith-family loyalty that

Jesus gives us as His followers could be summed up, "Blood is thicker than water, but the Holy Spirit is thicker than both!" Young adults need to know they are just as valued and loved as every other member of the family of God.

Engage young adults with the whole gospel to the whole person. Our church recently adopted a new mission statement: Engaging the whole person with the whole gospel of Jesus Christ—anywhere, anytime, and anyplace. It's no surprise that one of the groups in our church that have responded strongly to this mission is our young adults. Facing the complexities of a pluralistic culture and their own complicated journey into adulthood, they are famished for the depths of the gospel. Many grew up in churches where they heard a truncated or a one-dimensional version of the gospel. The ground-breaking book Soul Searching gave a specific and descriptive name to the watered-down version of Christianity that was being taught: moral therapeutic deism.[9] Many were never taught (if they were taught at all) as children and teenagers that being a disciple of Jesus means more than trying to be a "good person" as we wait to get to Heaven. Instead, young adults today are motivated to hear that we take seriously the commands of Jesus for the here and now. Not only that; they want their lives to matter, so they respond strongly to the idea of mission and specifically the call of the Great Commission (Matthew 28:18-20; John 20:21; Acts 1:8). For a generation that is largely rejecting the materialistic values of their parents and grandparents and looking for a chance to make a difference in the world, the full expression of the gospel inspires and motivates them. Instead of being scared off by some of the difficult teachings of the Bible, they instead embrace the challenge. I co-teach a mid-week Bible study that is aimed at pouring into developing leaders in our church called Coffeehouse Theology. I chose that name because I want to instill deep theological truths, but in a relaxed, conversational setting. One of our most consistent and engaged demographics in this study are our young adults who love the intergenerational makeup of the group and who ask some of the most thoughtful (and challenging) questions. Churches that are "growing young" aren't afraid to preach and teach the "whole gospel." Young adults resonate with less talk about abstract beliefs and more focus on the person and work of Jesus. They are less interested in "formulaic" messages (for example, "3 steps to...") and are more drawn to the redemptive meta-narrative of the Bible that orients them in a broken world. Finally, while young adults care about eternal life, they want to explore the new way of life that Jesus invites us to live out our faith in the present.[10]

Connect young adults with intergenerational biblical community that re-creates family. The community where I pastor is situated near one of the fastest growing cities in the United States. As people flood into middle Tennessee for the big-city-fun with small-city-charm, they realize they've been uprooted from their faith community (if they had one) and many are searching for a new one. One of the surprising reasons young adults choose our church family is not the excellent facility, good programs, or even the great preaching (ahem). Instead they love that they walk in the doors and see all generations— and in our very young community, senior adults specifically. Honestly, there are "cooler" churches all around us, so why would a stylish young adult choose us for their church home? The young adults that come to us are searching for more than a "church experience." They are looking for a surrogate family. They want to be around people from all generations and walks of life. Churches that reach young adults naturally will have some connecting points aimed at reaching young adults. But churches in which young adults flourish are integrating young adults into all levels of church life.

Young adults do seek community with each other and there are some groups comprised of primarily young adults in our church.

However, many of our small group Bible studies are intergenerational. In these groups, young men are being discipled by older men and younger women by older women (Titus 2:2-8). By the nature of their life stage, young adults are not always consistent with their schedules or their attendance. But even young adults rarely miss these disciple-making groups. The following is a statistic that stuns me every time I hear it or use it myself. If we want to know if someone will be a part of our church in five years, the single greatest leading indicator is their connection to a small group. Those in small groups are *five times* more likely to be active in the church than those who attend worship services alone.[11] "Warm is the new cool," and groups that experience life together draw young adults who crave biblical community. Relational warmth resonates with young adults. Many didn't grow up with biological fathers in the home, or were raised by an extended family member, or or are from homes filled with abuse and trauma. This type of biblical community goes beyond just being welcoming and elevates the value of true biblical hospitality. We should welcome young adults not only for meals, but into our lives. One of the comments we get consistently on our church-wide year-end survey, is *"this church feels like a family!"*

Empower young adults for significant leadership roles in the church. This is an era in which the demand for leadership greatly exceeds the supply. Signs of this imbalance are everywhere. Due to a variety of cultural shifts and competing demands for people's time, every organization of every kind is facing a leader shortage and our churches are no exception. Our ministries are usually led by middle-to-senior aged adults for good reasons: spiritual maturity and years of ministry experience. But there are only so many "seasoned veterans" to go around. In a surprising and welcome twist, sociologists note that retiring professionals and emerging adults share similar values but go about accomplishing them in very different ways. Retiring professionals were ready to change the world in the 1960s and 1970s, and they still strongly believe in causes. By the time millennials and Gen Z come of age, they could become the cleanest-cut young adults in living memory, known for their hard work on a grassroots reconstruction of community, teamwork, and civic spirit. Young adults are an untapped leadership resource who have time, creativity, and a passion to make a difference. Make sure you give them the vision and direction but don't micromanage them; their way of getting it done is probably more creative, more efficient, and more effective than yours.

Another key to developing young adults for ministry and leadership roles in the local church is the way in which they are led. This "new breed of leaders" don't want to be just your "volunteer;" they do want to discover a *calling*.[12] This generation doesn't really want to burn all their time checking their Snapchat and binge-watching Netflix, but most young adults are bored by the "vision" most leaders put before them. They don't just want to make a contribution; they want to make a *difference*. The phrase "just a volunteer" should have no place in our vocabulary as we reach out to young adults; there's a reason Chick-fil-A calls their well-trained and courteous employees "team members" with effective results.

Churches that don't develop young adults into leaders do so at their own peril. Churches need a clear leadership pipeline if you want to develop loyal and lasting leaders. A leadership pipeline is more than just a buzz phrase, it's essential to developing grassroots leaders who clearly know the standards and expectations for leadership at every level of the organization. Churches and organizations are learning in a post-institutional world that you don't just stumble upon great leaders; the best leaders are home-grown.

What you don't have to have. Many churches feel defeated before they get started because they have a preconceived notion of what it takes to reach young adults. This paradigm paralysis is mostly fueled by the old models we used to reach them as children and students. While it is true that most young adults prefer good coffee to bad and they do have preferences in the types of worship music played, if you look at the above platforms you'll notice that none of them are dependent on big churches, big budgets, or big buildings. One of the most refreshing things about today's young adults is that they've been marketed to so much that they are savvy and see through artificial attempts to gain their allegiance. They are much more drawn to authenticity and meaningful relationships. A church that has a desire to encourage young adults as full participants in the mission of the church, a church that is compassionate to the challenges they face, and a church that preaches the depths of the gospel while living out that mission as a faith family is what young adults are looking for more than pastors who wear skinny jeans or church décor made of reclaimed barn wood.

Measuring the New Norm

One of the greatest challenges in "recalibrating" ministry to young adults is that our normal metrics of measuring ministry success don't tell the whole story. As church leaders, we might preach kingdom impact, but we reward (and are usually rewarded) based on church growth. If we are going to recalibrate our ministries, we are going to have to "define the win" for young adults based on non-traditional metrics, relational methods of evaluating growth, and capturing trends through surveys and stories that illustrate what God is doing.

Develop a missional scorecard. Most churches have learned to talk a "good game" when it comes to kingdom priorities, but still try to measure their success by the numbers in their bulletin or on their annual report. Using traditional metrics to measure your impact with young adults can be particularly misleading: their attendance is inconsistent and their giving is almost non-existent. Churches that embrace mission over methods have learned to measure sending capacity and not just seating capacity. Author Reggie McNeal gives three shifts in missional thinking that must be translated into missional measures: from internal to external ministry focus; from program development to people development in terms of ministry activity; and from church-based to kingdom-based in terms of leadership agenda.[13]

While specific measures for each of these shifts must be contextualized for each church in each community, we can easily imagine some specific examples.

- Instead of how many young adults attended our evangelistic outreach service, how many gospel conversations did our young adults initiate outside of the church with the lost and searching in the past month?
- Instead of how many young adults attended a Bible study in the past month, what percentage of our young adults can name a spiritual mentor they meet with monthly?
- Instead of how many young adults are serving in our ministries within the church, how many young adults are serving with our strategic ministry partners outside of the church?

Use spiritual challenge questions. As our staff went through a recent evaluation of our ministry metrics, we realized that most of our measurements are what economists call "lagging" indicators. Lagging indicators are measurable factors that change only after the economy has begun to follow a particular pattern or trend. "Leading" indicators on the other hand are factors that change before the rest of the economy begins to go in a particular direction. Leading indicators aren't always as accurate or easy to capture as lagging indicators, but they allow you to "reverse engineer" a ministry strategy. We developed a set of "spiritual challenge" questions to be used in our disciple-making groups that we felt would be leading indicators of the spiritual depth, maturity, and mission. While many of our adults have struggled with this paradigm-shift, many of our young adults have embraced these five questions:

1. *How are you being changed by Jesus?* This question aims to measure our on-going spiritual transformation. It addresses spiritual health and growth and implies the use of the spiritual disciplines as people will share in response what they are learning through Bible study and in prayer.

2. *How are you being discipled and who are you discipling?* Every disciple of Jesus needs to be continually maturing and multiplying. It's been said that every growing follower of Jesus needs three types of relationships in their life: a Paul to mentor you, a Barnabas to encourage you, and a Timothy to invest in.

3. *When and where are you experiencing life-giving biblical community?* Acts 2:42-47 describes what Spirit-filled biblical community looks like but doesn't prescribe a program and strategy to accomplish it. This question allows for flexibility in *when* and *where,* but holds young adults accountable for making sure it is an important part of their spiritual rhythms.

4. *Who are the lost people you're praying for and having gospel conversations with?* We want to be intentional about cultivating relationships with the lost and equipping people to share the gospel. Praying for them keeps our spiritual sensitivity alert to opportunities to share the gospel (Matthew 9:35-38). We offer evangelism equipping and resources both in groups and through an app we developed for training and tracking gospel conversations.

5. *What is breaking your heart in the world and what are you doing about it?* Our young adults love this question because

they want to be a part of the solution to the many problems they see around them. The second part of the question is another way of asking, "Do we know our spiritual gifts and are we using them to serve?"

Craft surveys and capture stories. "How exactly are spiritual challenge questions also mission measures?" you might be asking. In other words, asking questions is great, but how do you know if they are working? We've discovered there are two primary ways: surveys and stories.

- **Surveys:** We create goals that hold us accountable as a ministry team to be sure these questions are working their way into our groups and the culture of our church. For example, "Equip 100% of group leaders in using the spiritual challenge questions and have 75% of groups using them every week by year end." There are other questions we ask on our year-end surveys as well that are helpful such as: (1) How often per week are you talking about faith outside of church groups and activities? (2) How often per week do you have a faith talk or Bible study in your place of residence? and (3) How many times in the last month did you serve someone outside of the church?

- **Stories:** Pastor Chris Brooks, who leads the largest young adult ministry at any of our ministry campuses, shared there are three types of stories that our leaders are learning to identify and document as "gospel breakthroughs." The first type of story is career decisions. When young adults bring workplace choices before their group leader and peers to ask for prayer and wise counsel, that is a sign they are learning to making Jesus Lord over their work life. Second, many young adults are learning vulnerability for the first time in group life. If the leaders hear the phrase, *"I've never told anyone this before…"* it's a sign they are reaching a new level of trust and seeking healing. Finally, a sign they are grasping the "whole gospel" is their ability to start interpreting events in their lives, both good and bad, through the lens of Scripture.

Summary

Young adults today face unprecedented challenges as they transition into adulthood, establish meaningful relationships, and attempt to discover a direction and purpose for their lives. Sadly, most young adults are absent from our churches during these crucial moments of their lives. Churches have ignored or neglected the needs of emerging adults assuming it's a "gap" to mature adulthood. It doesn't have to be this way. Churches of any shape or size that see young adults as an important part of the faith family, preach the whole gospel, cultivate community, and equip them as leaders will not only reach and retain young adults, but will strengthen the entire church. Churches must recalibrate ministry to young adults based on a "new scorecard" that measures missional impact, asks good leading questions, and sees a culture shift based on surveys and stories.

Resources to Explore Further

- *Growing Young: 6 Essential Strategies to Help Young People Discover and Love Your Church* by Brad Griffin, Jake Mulder, and Kara Powell.
- *Gaining by Losing: Why the Future Belongs to Churches That Send* by J. D. Greear.
- *Missional Renaissance: Changing the Scorecard for the Church* by Reggie McNeal.

Endnotes

[1] J.D. Grear, Gaining By Losing: Why the Future Belongs to Churches That Send, (Grand Rapids, MI: Zondervan, 2015), 45.

[2] http://nationalmarriageproject.org/wp-content/uploads/2013/03/KnotYet-FinalForWeb.pdf.

[3] Robert Schoeni and Karen Ross, "Material Assistance From Families During the Transition to Adulthood," In On the Frontier of Adulthood: Theory, Research, and Public Policy, (Chicago, IL: The University of Chicago Press, 2008), 396-416.

[4] Kara Powell, Jake Mulder, and Brad Griffin. Growing Young: Six Essential Strategies to Help People Discover and Love Your Church, (Grand Rapids, MI: Baker Books, 2016), 15-16.

[5] Mark Chavez, "American Congregations at the Beginning of the 21st Century: A National Congregations Study," http://www.soc.duke.edu/natcong/Docs/NCSII_report_final.pdf.

[6] David Kinnaman and Aly Hawkins, You Lost Me, (Grand Rapids, MI: Baker House, 2011), 23.

[7] Aaron Earls, Young Adults Keep Christian Label, but Fewer "devout." Baptist Press, posted Thursday, January 31, 2019. http://www.bpnews.net/52337/young-adults-keep-christian-label-but-fewer-devout.

[8] For more about our young adult ministry, see "A Moment in Time: Authentic Young Adult Ministry as it Happens" by Mike Glenn, (Nashville, TN: B&H, 2009) or visit kairosnashville.com.

[9] Christian Smith and Melinda Lundquist Denton, Soul Searching: The Religious and Spiritual Lives of American Teenagers, (New York, NY: Oxford University Press, 2005), 162-163.

[10] Powell, 126.

[11] https://thomrainer.com/2015/04/five-organizational-reasons-many-churches-hit-attendance-plateaus/.

[12] Jonathan McKee and Thomas W. McKee, The New Breed: Understanding and Equipping the 21st Century Volunteer, (Colorado Springs, CO: Group Publishing, 2002), 23.

[13] Reggie McNeil, Missional Renaissance: Changing the Scorecard for the Church, (San Francisco, CA: Jossey-Bass, 2009), xvi.

8
Youth Ministry in Thirds

Richard Ross

We are to grow up in all aspects into Him
who is the head, even Christ…
Ephesians 4:15b (NASB)

If most youth pastors were to stop doing about two-thirds of their tasks, churches might begin producing more lifetime disciples of Jesus. Why? Because if they stop doing less important work, then they will have time to do other things that offer even more promise. The principles of this chapter easily apply to children's, preschool, college, and other categories of specific ministry leaders within your church. If you are not serving with youth, just mark through the word youth and write your ministry area over it.

Current Unhealthy Norms

Many youth ministry leaders have grown up in programmatic, high activity, busy youth ministries. The youth area featured many games, attractive furnishings, and technology. Relationships with each other may have been the most remembered value rather than with King Jesus. Teenagers who only connect with peers and a few youth leaders generally will not walk in faith in adulthood. Those who spend their teenage years with multiple heart connections with believers of all ages—and those who serve King Jesus with believers of all ages—

probably will. That fact is sobering given the high percentage who spend their teenage years living in a youth ministry bubble at church.

Most teenagers who leave high school with little love for the Bride eventually will wander away from the Groom.

Well meaning youth pastors tend to minister the way they were led unless they find meaning and value to change. A great example of doing what we always have surfaced when my son, Clayton, and I were coming home from church after a mission trip meeting. Many of the youth were getting ready to leave in a couple of days and this meeting dealt with last minute packing and travel instructions. As we drove home, Clayton asked if I thought the closing prayer time was concerning. I asked him to explain further. He recalled the closing prayer time that went something like the typical prayer around such events, "Father help us to minister effectively, protect our kids from sickness, help all flights to go smoothly, keep them away from dangerous situations, and let everything go smoothly on this trip." Clayton insightfully asked, "Dad, does that sound like we just prayed Jesus out of the equation? We asked that things go so well that Christ does not even need to show up in the difficult situations that teach us the most."

Ministry tends to continue modeling what we have done in the past, but it is a great time to ask what should be different. Research shows that out of all the youth in your ministry, nearly half will stop attending church, struggle with their faith, and potentially half of them may never return to church again. If that is our normal trend, why is the church not bothered enough to say, "enough is enough, this has to change!" Part of the problem comes from the expectations of the parents who have youth in your ministry.

Spiritually lethargic parents suck the power from youth ministry. Spiritually alive parents intensify the youth ministry. Spiritually lethargic parents create spiritually lethargic young adults. Spiritually alive parents create young disciples who join King Jesus in changing the world.

The following might be an exaggeration, but some church parents seem to have these "discipleship" goals for their church's youth ministry:

- Make church so fun that my Precious will come without giving me hassle at home.
- Motivate sweet Precious to succeed and make a good living.
- Keep my Precious from doing the big sins that would embarrass me.

Churches can temporarily build attendance by keeping teenagers in the youth bubble and by allowing entertainment to overshadow service and ministry. (After all, for fifty years we have conditioned teenagers to embrace fun and peers.) But the research is irrefutable. Such an approach will lead to a high percentage of those "great crowds" walking away from the church after high school. Who would call that successful youth ministry? Youth ministry authority Walt Mueller says:

> It is ironic that one of the marks of today's emerging generations is a deep need for community and connectedness, and yet we plan and program in ways that cut them off from experiencing community and connectedness with people who aren't their own age. It's also ironic that while we say we want to see our kids embrace Jesus and mature into a deep faith that's integrated into all of life, we separate them from the wisest and most seasoned members of the body.[1]

Recalibrate to a New Norm

The great majority of youth pastors love King Jesus supremely, embrace their calling fully, and do their work tirelessly. But the time has come for their workweeks to change.

Though their numbers are not great, twenty-something disciples do exist. Those walking in faith, loving the church, and making a difference in the world tend to share three characteristics:

- They were reared by parents who adored Jesus, loved the church, and were on mission to see Christ's Kingdom come on earth.
- They grew up with a rich web of relationships with the full congregation and were on mission with church members of all ages.
- They were in a Bible-drenched youth group led by a youth pastor and leaders who carried the aroma of Jesus.

This chapter (and this book) presents a strong biblical case for ministering to teenagers through families, in concert with the full body of Christ, and in age-specific programming. The voice of Scripture outweighs any other considerations. But it is interesting to note that the most reliable studies regarding lifetime faith coalesce around these same three arenas.

We now know the three arenas of ministry most likely to lead to lifetime disciples. Therefore, forward-thinking youth pastors might consider the following workweeks:

- Approximately fifteen hours a week accelerating the spiritual impact of the homes where his teenagers live.
- Approximately fifteen hours a week immersing every teenager in the full life and ministry of the congregation.
- Approximately fifteen hours a week leading what we traditionally have considered youth ministry.

For the more visually inclined, consider it this way:

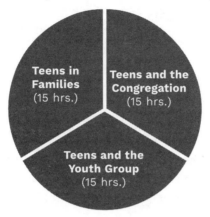

Of course, ministry is never that neat and tidy time-wise. But these broad hourly divisions point to a significant shift in the youth pastor's role. The fifteen-hour blocks include administrative planning, public leadership, and one-on-one ministry. Each of these three arenas of ministry merits attention.

Accelerate the spiritual impact of parents. One or two parent seminars a year will not motivate parents to begin spiritually leading at home. But fifteen hours a week can give the youth pastor time to:

- Partner with the other church leaders to deepen the parents' walk with Jesus.
- Call out and teach parents how to lead spiritually at home.
- Equip them to parent biblically.
- Partner with other church leaders to introduce lost parents to Jesus.

Immersing every teenager in the full life and ministry of the congregation. Dan Dupee says to Christian parents:

> Strong families are the starting point, but not the ending point. The ending point is the body of Christ, since "from

123

whom the whole body, being fitted and held together by what every joint supplies, according to the proper working of each individual part, causes the growth of the body for the building up of itself in love" (Ephesians 4:16). Your kids need to see that other respectable grown-ups are as crazy about Jesus as their parents.[2]

In both the Old and New Testaments, God's people usually appear in intergenerational relationships. "O God, You have taught me from my youth, and I still declare Your wondrous deeds. And even when *I am* old and gray, O God, do not forsake me, Until I declare Your strength to *this* generation, Your power to all who are to come" (Psalm 71:17-18, NASB).

Youth pastors need to do fresh thinking about ways churches can use buildings, budgets, and calendars to create rich webs of relationships around every child, teenager, and adult. One result might be young adults who love Christ's church and who consider the full congregation to be family. Dupee adds, "It lends power and credibility to the gospel message when…children see it embraced by people for whom they have affection and respect and who they know are genuinely interested not only in Jesus but in them."[3]

A youth ministry book that has sparked conversation is Chap Clark's *Adoptive Youth Ministry*. He makes a strong case for teenagers and members of the congregation adopting each other. Clark believes teenagers have much to give as well as receive, so he calls for mutual adoption.

Paul is the only New Testament writer to use the term *adoption* (*huiothesia*). God the Father adopts believers into His eternal family, and He intends for these "siblings" to live in warm unity. Even more importantly, He intends for the generations to link arms and serve the Kingdom of Christ together. A youth pastor might ask teenagers:

- Not counting relatives and youth workers, how many adults in our church know your name, know interesting things about you, and often show interest in your life?
- Not counting relatives, how many children in our church would say you are important to them relationally and spiritually?

A youth pastor could dramatically change the answers to these questions by spending fifteen hours a week:

- Multiplying mutual adoptions between teenagers and all ages of believers.
- Calling out and equipping every teenager to take places of Kingdom service with children or adults.

Connecting teens to the other adults in the church takes intentionality. The first step may be simply merging events or activities that already occur. You do not need to invent new activities, just include multiple generations in the ones you already have.

Leading traditional youth ministry. Grade-schoolers need to search Scripture to find how to imitate Jesus on a recess playground. Senior adults need to search the Word to discover new ways to be on mission after retirement. Age-specific ministry is a valuable part of church life.

Mark Cannister notes, "There is a strong consensus among intergenerational specialists that while the church embraces intergenerational values, it is also essential to maintain important age-specific ministries."[4] The research project reported in the book *Why They Stay* found that "a young adult who attended a church with a ministry to students was more likely to have stayed as an adult, and one who attended a church without a ministry to students was more likely to have strayed."[5]

Mobilize teenagers to perform the functions of the church (evangelism, worship, discipleship, ministry, and community), while

125

linking arms with their peers and youth leaders. Churches should celebrate:

- The youth pastor who presents text-driven talks relevant to the specific issues of the teenage years.
- Open-group Bible study that presents foundational concepts to all teenagers.
- Intensive discipleship for those specific teenagers who have made a clear decision to follow Jesus.
- Groups of teenagers who move out to evangelize and make disciples locally and globally.
- Teenagers developing community. Warm friendships and laughter are part of what King Jesus was promising in John 10:10.

Ministry built around thirds still provides time for youth worship, open-group Bible study, intensive discipleship, evangelistic and caring outreach, and fellowship. Time is also well-spent on a few special youth events, but only those that are strategic to creating lifetime disciples. Programing that does not contribute to lifetime faith has to go away.

The motivation for ministry in thirds. Gratitude and adoration toward King Jesus provide the motivation for youth ministry. Veteran youth leader Rodger Nishioka says, "The doctrine of grace serves as a key theological basis for youth ministry because [teenagers], more than people at any other age, desperately need to know they are loved for who they are without ties to performance or condition."[6]

Grace flows from the Gospel. Pastor and author J.D. Greear puts it this way:

The gospel is that Christ has suffered the full wrath of God for my sin... Second Corinthians 5:21 says that He actually became my sin so that I could literally become His

126

righteousness... When I receive that grace in repentance and faith, full acceptance becomes mine... That means that God could not love me any more than He does right now, because God could not love and accept Christ any more than He does, and God sees me in Christ.[7]

Romans 5:18-19 says: "So then as through one transgression there resulted condemnation to all men, even so through one act of righteousness there resulted justification of life to all men. For as through the one man's disobedience the many were made sinners, even so through the obedience of the One the many will be made righteous" (NASB).

When teenagers grasp this, the discovery will be life-changing for them. Young followers of Christ often have a hard time understanding forgiveness and live with shame, typically because grace has not been modeled at home. Leaders might teach them that God sees them in Christ and then ask: "When God looks at His Son, how much sin does He see? When God looks at you in His Son, how much sin does He see?"

For teenagers, grasping grace will lead to gratitude. Nishioka says, "Grace is completely unexpected. There is no logic and no reason as to why God, who is the maker of the universe, should love us so incredibly that God would send Jesus to die for us."[8]

Swindoll explains the results of grace when he says:

All who embrace grace become "free indeed." Free from what? Free from oneself. Free from guilt and shame. Free from the damnable impulses I couldn't stop when I was in bondage to sin. Free from the tyranny of others' opinions, expectations, demands. And free to what? Free to obey. Free to love. Free to forgive others as well as myself... Free to serve and glorify Christ.[9]

What motivates teenagers toward such obedience? Greear says:

> Those people who get better are those who understand that God's approval of them is not dependent on their getting better... Abiding in Jesus will produce all of the fruits of the Spirit in you—but not by having you concentrate particularly on any of those things. You concentrate on Jesus. You rest in His love and acceptance, given to you not because of what you have earned, but because of what He has earned for you.[10]

Perhaps all this helps youth leaders envision a ministry filled with believers grateful for grace and hearts full of adoration towards their King. Swindoll says:

> Fortunately, grim, frowning, joyless saints in Scripture are conspicuous by their absence. Instead, the examples I find are of adventurous, risk-taking, enthusiastic, and authentic believers whose joy was contagious even in times of painful trial... The contrast between then and now is staggering. The difference, I am convinced, is grace.[11]

Grace-filled relationships within the body of Christ are wonderful, but they are not the end of the story. David Platt lifts eyes to the bigger picture when he says, "Enjoy his grace and extend his glory. This is the twofold purpose behind the creation of the human race... God blesses his people with extravagant grace so they might extend his extravagant glory to all people of the earth."[12]

The big picture. The diagram on page 129 illustrates youth ministry in thirds. The terms that make up this diagram deserve careful consideration.

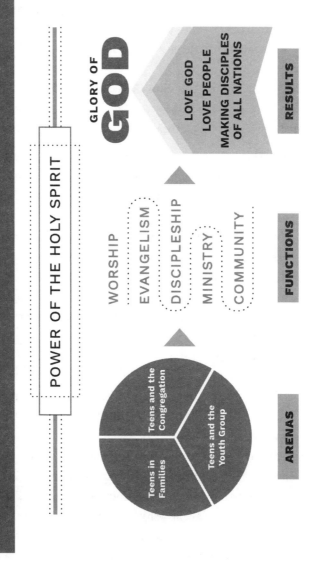

YOUTH MINISTRY THAT LASTS A LIFETIME

POWER OF THE HOLY SPIRIT

GLORY OF
GOD

LOVE GOD
LOVE PEOPLE
MAKING DISCIPLES
OF ALL NATIONS

RESULTS

WORSHIP
EVANGELISM
DISCIPLESHIP
MINISTRY
COMMUNITY

FUNCTIONS

Teens and the
Congregation

Teens in
Families

Teens and the
Youth Group

ARENAS

The power of the Holy Spirit. Jesus said: "Abide in Me, and I in you. As the branch cannot bear fruit of itself unless it abides in the vine, so neither *can* you unless you abide in Me. I am the vine, you are the branches; he who abides in Me and I in him, he bears much fruit, for apart from Me *you can do nothing*" (John 15:4-5, emphasis added).

The functions of the church. Many individuals, churches, and groups have similar views of the five functions of the local church. Many believers would embrace the following definitions:

- **Worship**—Worship is any activity in which believers experience God in a meaningful, spiritually transforming way. Encountering God in worship transforms us more and more into His likeness.[13]

- **Evangelism**—Evangelism is believers sharing the Gospel with lost persons. Evangelism is asking them to repent of their sins, to put their faith in Christ for the forgiveness of sins and the free gift of eternal life, and to follow Him forever as Lord. Evangelism is the good news spoken by believers and lived out in their lives.

- **Discipleship**—Discipleship is a process that begins with their conversion and continues throughout a believer's life. Discipleship occurs when one believer engages another and the result is that both become more Christlike in what they think and do.

- **Ministry**—Ministry is meeting another person's need in the name of Jesus. Ministry grows out of a transformed and serving life. Ministry is the normal function of every believer.

- **Community** (or Fellowship)—Community is person-to-person relationships. Churches tend to have the kind of fellowship they want and our Lord expects when they focus on evangelism, discipleship, ministry, and worship.

The Results. God intends that the functions of the church (and individuals and families) will lead to the fulfillment of the Great Commandment and the Great Commission. In other words, He intends that the church will:

- Love God.
- Love people.
- Make disciples of all nations.

The Great Commandment is taken from Matthew 22:35-39: "One of them, a lawyer, asked Him a question, testing Him, 'Teacher, which is the great commandment in the Law?' And He said to him, 'You shall love the Lord your God with all your heart, and with all your soul, and with all your mind.' This is the great and foremost commandment. The second is like it, 'You shall love your neighbor as yourself'" (NASB).

The Great Commission is taken from Matthew 28:18-20, "And Jesus came up and spoke to them, saying, 'All authority has been given to Me in heaven and on earth. Go therefore and make disciples of all the nations, baptizing them in the name of the Father and the Son and the Holy Spirit, teaching them to observe all that I commanded you; and lo, I am with you always, even to the end of the age'" (NASB).

The ultimate outcome. A Christ-follower exists for the glory of God. A family exists for the glory of God. A youth ministry and a church exist for the glory of God. God's Word is crystal clear (emphasis added):

- "Therefore, having been justified by faith, we have peace with God through our Lord Jesus Christ, through whom also we have obtained our introduction by faith into this grace in which we stand; and we exult in hope of *the glory of God*" (Romans 5:1-2, NASB).

131

- "Whether, then, you eat or drink or whatsoever you do, do all to *the glory of God*" (1 Corinthians 10:31, NASB).
- "For all things are for your sakes, so that the grace which is spreading to more and more people may cause the giving of thanks to abound to *the glory of God*" (2 Corinthians 4:15, NASB).
- "For this reason also, God highly exalted Him, and bestowed on Him the name which is above every name, so that at the name of Jesus every knee will bow, of those who are in heaven and on earth and under the earth, and that every tongue will confess that Jesus Christ is Lord, to the *glory of God* the Father" (Philippians 2:9-11, NASB).

Guiding the church toward youth ministry in thirds. Of course, a youth pastor who implements youth ministry in thirds on his own will soon be unemployed. Well-meaning senior pastors, church leaders, parents, and even teenagers think they are "paying" the youth pastor to provide programming for teenagers. Period. Without preparation, youth pastors could face parents who go ballistic when they think they are losing their babysitting service. And the teenagers may only see this as trading the Xboxes for "old people who smell weird."

Slow and careful change seems much wiser. Movement in new directions might follow this flow:

- The senior pastor, youth pastor, and core church leaders pore over Scripture, pray deeply, and draft a direction for the future.
- That group invites leadership staff, core parents, core leaders, core teenagers, and core congregation members to speak into, adjust, and then affirm the direction.
- Leaders present the plan to the full church and youth group.
- The church creates ongoing ways to celebrate, affirm, and tangibly reward the youth pastor as he takes the lead in new directions.

As noted before, the great majority of our youth pastors love King Jesus supremely, embrace their calling fully, and do their work tirelessly. But by doing those things the church expects them to do, the great majority of church teenagers are not becoming world-changing disciples as adults.

Everyone knows the definition of *insanity*.

Clearly the time to move toward change is now.

Measuring the New Norm

A lifetime of study of Scripture, digesting research, and observing high school graduates lead this author to humbly suggest the top ten most important factors that provide measurables in developing a lifetime faith. The list presupposes a relationship with Jesus.

1. Do you observe teenagers who share a warm heart connection with a parent who is transparent about his or her adoration of God's Son, who embraces God's written Word, and who lives for the glory of God?

2. Are your teenagers sharing a life-on-life relationship with a disciple who adores Jesus and guides the teenager through a challenging, systematic discipleship process?

3. Do the teenagers in your church share heart connections with many members of the congregation and do they share a mutual "adoption" with one or more adults who adore Jesus?

4. Do your teenagers actively serve and minister with other generations as well as peers?

5. Do your teenagers actively participate in intergenerational worship on Sunday mornings?

6. Do your teenagers know how to correctly interpret Scripture and to pray, and do they take responsibility for their own spiritual growth?

7. Are the teenagers in your church confident about having conversations that are evangelistic or that call for a reasoned defense of the faith?

8. Do the teenagers know how to apply the principles of Scripture to their lives while navigating a pluralistic culture?

9. Do your teenagers approach vocation and all of life with a sense of divine calling and an appreciation for their spiritual gifts?

10. Do your teenagers connect with significant adults who welcome and work together on their doubts and questions?

Resources to Explore Further

- *Youth Ministry That Lasts a Lifetime* by Richard Ross (this chapter is adapted from this work with permission).
- *Growing Young: Six Essential Strategies to Help Young People Discover and Love Your Church* by Kara Powell, Jake Mulder, and Brad Griffin.
- *Parenting Teens: Essentials for the Journey* by Richard Ross and David Booth.
- *31 Truths to Shape Your Youth Ministry* by Richard Ross and Gus Reyes.
- *Parent Checkup: Seeing Through the Eyes of Your Teenager* (mom and dad editions) by Richard Ross.
- *Youth Ministry in the 21st Century: Five Views* by Chap Clark.

Endnotes

[1] https://cpyu.org/2018/06/29/why-youth-ministry-shouldnt-be-the-greatest-show-on-earth-2/.

[2] Dan Dupee, It's Not Too Late (Grand Rapids, MI: Baker Books, 2016), 109.

[3] Ibid., 110.

[4] Mark Cannister, Teenagers Matter: Making Student Ministry a Priority in the Church (Grand Rapids, MI: Baker Academic, 2013), 139.

[5] Steve R. Parr and Tom Crites, Why They Stay: Helping Parents and Church Leaders Make Investments That Keep Children and Teens Connected to the Church for a Lifetime (Bloomington, IN: WestBow Press, 2015), 105.

[6] Rodger Nishioka, "Theological Foundation for Youth Ministry: Grace" in Starting Right: Thinking Theologically About Youth Ministry, eds. Kenda Dean, Chap Clark, and Dave Rahn (Grand Rapids, MI: Zondervan, 2001), 249.

[7] J.D. Greear, Gospel: Recovering the Power That Made Christianity Revolutionary (Nashville, TN: B&H Publishing Group, 2011), 46-47.

[8] Nishioka, Starting Right, 246.

[9] Charles R. Swindoll, Grace Awakening (Nashville, TN: Thomas Nelson, 2003), 40-41.

[10] Greear, Gospel, 14.

[11] Swindoll, Grace Awakening, 279.

[12] David Platt, Radical (Colorado Springs, CO: Multnomah Press, 2010), 65, 69.

[13] Gene Mims, Kingdom Principles for Church Growth (Nashville, TN: LifeWay Christian Resources, 1994), 34-57.

9
The Future Steps of Our Children

Lydia Randall

Can I be honest? I envisioned starting this chapter with a warm cup of tea in my favorite local coffee shop—snuggled up with my laptop. The reality is that I just put my oldest child in bed for the fourth time tonight and my youngest came home from school sick with a stomach bug. I did not make it to the fabulous coffee shop. You and I, and every other parent have these beautiful pictures of life, of being a parent, of family life and our wonderfully behaved children that are growing in Christ—but the reality often looks entirely different. And that is where we have to meet our parents—in their reality, where their aspirations are sidelined because of interrupted and overloaded schedules, plans that don't go accordingly and kids that don't cooperate in our grand scheme of things. It is in the imperfect, in the every day. We have the privilege and the incredible calling to help parents not be perfect, but be intentional. But how do we accomplish that?

We are a generation that outsources everything. We outsource our laundry, the cleaning of our homes, and the mowing of our lawns. Unfortunately, many parents are also outsourcing the spiritual development of their children to the church. It is not the church's job to be the primary disciple-makers for our children. The church does have a job. The job of the church is to cast vision for a biblical picture of the home. But we have to do more than just cast vision—we are called to help walk alongside and equip our parents for their vital mission.

Current Unhealthy Norms

Most parents say one, if not both, of two things. First, they feel overwhelmed, and second, they feel ill-equipped.

Overwhelmed. We live in a fast-paced, social media driven and sports involved culture that is driving and overwhelming so many of our families today. As a result, many Christian parents are more concerned with their kids excelling in sports and academics and only hoping for the best spiritually. Worst case scenario, spiritual formation is not even on the parents' radar. Even parents who are aware of spiritual development are often outsourcing to the church. A mom recently commented, "If I can just keep the kids clean and fed, can the church take care of all that spiritual stuff?" With so many demands pulling for our families attention, parents are often overwhelmed with the day-to-day activities and schedules for their kids. So, then comes the church with the reminder that God designed parents to be the primary disciple-makers and we get a deer in headlights response. We must do more than just proclaim the mandate from God—that they are the parents and they cannot outsource this God-given role. We must help them understand that God never asks us to do something without also providing the resources to accomplish the mission. Remind them of the privilege and joy they have in this opportunity to disciple their child and that their church is a willing partner to help them do what only they can do.

As ministry leaders, we often feel overwhelmed ourselves and don't have the bandwidth to add anything else to our already full plate or budget. We have to adopt a plan that not only works and is easy for our parents, but also works and is easy for us to implement. We don't need another program or event to fill this great need we see, which can be more taxing on church staff and volunteers. The difficulty with adding another event or program "at the church" is that we lose the majority of our families. We have to try to engage the parent who will never show up at the church for a parenting event because of their schedule, the sports tournaments, or because they are afraid someone might ask them about something they cannot know the answer. It is often the families that are already excited and engaged in passing their faith that show up for these events. It is not what is not happening at church that is the problem. It is what is not happening at home. We have to get these tools and resources to equip our parents IN THE HOME. By getting training for parents in the privacy of their own homes, we can also provide a way for parents to learn and grow in their own journey in a less threatening way. This is a significant paradigm shift, to put time, budget, or personnel into something that is not going to be taking place at the church. We have to take steps to resource and equip at home. We must provide home-centric resources with clear steps to follow. When we do, the parents will gain confidence they can accomplish what God has called them to do. We can help, but we can't do their job for them.

Ill-equipped. Even some of the best-intended parents do not feel comfortable passing faith to their children, because they do not feel confident in their own faith. They may not be passing their faith and teaching their children about spiritual disciplines because they do not currently know how to practice those disciplines or were never taught those growing up. Many of our parents are first generation believers or new believers who may struggle significantly in this area. Many parents do not yet have a picture of what the Christian life looks like. They are afraid that their child will ask them a question they do not know how to answer. As the church, we must provide encouragement, resources, and tools to make it easy and likely that they will grow first in their own personal relationship and walk with the Lord and then have a dynamic faith to pass to the next generation.

In Deuteronomy 6:7-8 it says, "Impress them on your children. Talk about them when you sit at home and when you walk along the road, when you lie down and when you get up. Tie them as symbols on your hands and bind them on your foreheads. Write them on the doorframes of your houses and on your gates" (NIV). What rich and clear teaching God has given us for parents to disciple their children. But we have to go back and start at verses 5-6, "Love the Lord your God with all your heart and with all your soul and with all your strength. These commandments that I give you today are to be on your hearts" (NIV). We cannot give what we do not possess. Our first job is to help our parents grow in their own relationship with Christ so their children can experience the overflow and see His work in mom and dad.

We have an enemy, and he wants to convince our parents they are not equipped and do not have enough knowledge and wisdom to disciple their children. As Christian leaders, we must remind them of who they are in Him and they have the Holy Spirit inside of them to guide them. If God has called them to it, He will equip them for it. They have access to the same power that raised Jesus Christ from the dead. We can help give the parents confidence by declaring what the Word says. God has called us and will equip us. Give parents a vision and speak His truth over them. In James 1:5, it says that if we lack wisdom, we should ask God and that He will give it generously. Remind parents that first and foremost they need wisdom from their Heavenly Father, who wants to give it to them in abundance. They are responsible to disciple their children and God will provide them with everything they need to carry out this call.

The book of Genesis reminds us that God created the home before He created the church. It has always been His plan for the home to be the center of spiritual formation. The church is a part of that, but the church needs to understand its role. It is our job to help these parents and give them a picture of what this can look like. Show them how this looks in the context of everyday busy family life. Give them a picture of passing faith that demonstrates to their children not a list of to-do's, but one that is full of life and adventure in connection with a living God that has purpose and hope for them.

We must first help parents see the most beautiful calling of being disciple-makers of their own children. But it goes well beyond this vision casting. We must also help equip our parents so they can know how to walk this faith journey with their children. "I get it. But now what?" As I sat across from this couple, they got it—they were all in and had caught the vision that God had called them to be the primary disciple maker for the kids He entrusted to them. There was an excitement, as they felt a great call and purpose. And then it all changed—the excitement seemed to turn to a sudden panic as I heard the next words that would follow… "But now what? What do I do today with a four-year-old? How do I get them from birth to inviting Christ to be their Lord and Savior to launching them as a fully developing follower of Christ? What do I do today?"

Recalibrate to a New Norm

As a new mom, I remember being inundated with charts and schedules I needed to follow to give my child the best chance to thrive. There were charts for growing physically—weight, height, and even head circumference. Colorful graphs showed me when my child should be walking and talking—how many words they should be saying at different ages and stages. But there seemed to be very little to help me make sure my child was thriving spiritually—and really this is the most critical aspect of my child's life. This would have eternal significance for my child.

141

What if we could provide similar guidance to parents to help their child's faith journey? Not a legalistic to-do list, but a healthy guide of intentionality. Most parents genuinely do want to be intentional, but unless they have a plan, they are not likely to follow through. We need to equip our parents with an in-home discipleship path, giving predictable stages they can prepare for and be proactive in their child's journey.

How can we be more effective in training our parents to feel confident to pass faith along? When we give a clear path, a plan, we make it easy and more likely for them to follow through. Give parents one specific thing to focus on for just this one year for one child. If we give too much or are too broad or don't go beyond vision casting, parents will often try to do everything and will end up doing nothing. We need to walk alongside parents to guide their child's spiritual journey one step at a time. The tendency is to overload parents when giving such vision, but be deliberate with practical tools and resources for the "today" for our parents.

By connecting specific ages to certain milestones and related spiritual disciplines, we help parents focus on the next stage of their child's spiritual development. For example, a child will be learning to read around the age of seven. This is the prime time for a parent to put special attention and focus with their child on reading the Bible, learning Scripture, and the importance of God's Word. We can use these predictable opportunities and pair them with certain ages for the most significant impact on a child's spiritual journey. This is not to say that a parent does not teach about the truth of God's Word until a child turns seven. This does mean that a parent ought to be aware of the optimal opportunity available at this age to guide their seven year old to feel comfortable navigating and learning about the Bible in a more personal way. This also helps the well-meaning parents to have a plan of not just hoping they get around to teaching these spiritual disciplines sometime and then unintentionally forgetting. Give parents a clear path coordinating with ages to guide their child's spiritual journey one step at a time. And then give them training for each step—including biblical insight for that season, teaching on that step, practical tools to put into action, and recommended resources for going further. When parents are equipped with the right tools at the right time, discipleship in the home is much more likely to happen and have a lasting impact. When tools help create an environment in the home for a strong foundation, close relationships, building trust, and having fun together—faith is more likely to stick. What are those predictable opportunities? Although not an exhaustive list, below are suggestions of significant upcoming steps that includes both spiritual disciplines and milestones for parents to focus on and prepare for intentionally.

Spiritual journey one step at a time: spiritual disciplines and milestones. Spiritual disciplines are those practices found in Scripture that promote spiritual growth in Jesus Christ. They are habits of devotion that become part of the fabric of our lives. A spiritual discipline can be any activity that helps you to grow your reliance upon Jesus.

Our children are not going to become spiritually strong by coincidence—just like they would not become physically strong by coincidence. Certain activities or disciplines help them to grow physically strong—such as the foods they eat, the exercise they partake in, and the sleep they get. In the same way, certain activities or disciplines will help our children grow spiritually strong. It is our job to help our parents identify these so they can help their children grow spiritually strong.

Spiritual disciplines or practices are holy habits that draw us close to the Lord. They help us grow in truth and direct us in our journey with Him. Although not a complete list, growth can include the following:

- **Prayer:** Prayer is how we communicate and connect to our Heavenly Father. Nurture your child's faith by praying together as a family as soon as they are born and by guiding them in the practice of praying individually. Suggested Age: 6
- **Bible Study:** Teach your child about God's Word and establish the practice of reading and memorizing Scripture as a family. Trusting the Holy Spirit—inspired words of Scripture as our guide, wisdom, and strength for life. (Related disciplines include Bible study, Scripture meditation, and praying God's Word.) Suggested Age: 7
- **Worship:** Practice adoring God personally, at home, at church, together as a family and as a lifestyle. Worship is our response to the greatness of God. We need to help our children understand that worship involves much more than attending a weekend service. We can worship God privately or in community. Suggested Age: 8
- **Serving/Giving:** Establish the practice of giving and serving others for God's glory. Humbly serving God by overflowing with His love and compassion to others, especially those in need. (Also including tithing and spiritual gifts.) Suggested Age: 9

A milestone is an action or event that marks a significant change or a particular stage in development. Scripture shows us the significance of celebrating spiritual steps. God's people set aside time to celebrate the spiritual passages in their lives. Parents can do many things to make lasting spiritual impressions on their children. Something as easy as setting aside time and having a simple celebration can give honor and significance to the spiritual markers that occur in each child's life. If we can help parents be prepared for upcoming stages and milestones, they can be proactive instead of reactive. Preparing for certain stages and milestones gives parents the confidence to walk with their child during times of change and cultivates a relationship in times of celebration.

This can include the following:

- **Prepare to Lead Your Child to Christ:** Parents are often overwhelmed with the task of leading their child to Christ. Many times, their child wants to get baptized, and the parents are so excited, but have never talked with their child about asking Jesus into their life to forgive their sins and lead their life. We need to equip our parents with how to have these conversations. This is usually a process for most children. If we can train our parents, then when their child begins to ask questions, they are equipped for these conversations to talk about inviting Christ to be both their Lord and Savior. As a church leader, we want to include the parents as much as possible in the most important decision their child will ever make. (Side note—for us, this has meant more faith decisions are happening at home instead of the church. We need to address this and celebrate this shift.) Suggested Age: 5

- **Salvation:** Celebrate your child's faith decision of making a personal, individual decision to ask Jesus Christ to be their Savior and Lord. Make this an annual celebration as you acknowledge their spiritual birthday! Take time to talk through how they have grown spiritually in the last year and lead them toward growing in their faith in the year to come. Suggested Age: Age will vary

- **Baptism:** Baptism is a public announcement of belief and a visible picture of an inward transformation. All who experience God's saving grace and respond through faith in Jesus Christ for forgiveness should be baptized in obedience to Jesus' command as recorded in the New Testament. Parents help your child understand there is nothing magical about the water and being baptized is not what makes them a Christian. Becoming a Christian is the decision to ask Jesus Christ to forgive their sins and take control of their life. Baptism is obeying Jesus' instruction after a salvation decision. Suggested Age: Age will vary

- **Preparing For Adolescence:** Discuss the changes and challenges of puberty in a proactive and positive way by talking about bodily changes, decision-making, and the changing relationship with you. Suggested Age: 10 or 11
- **Purity:** Give a vision for God-honoring thoughts and actions. Purity is much more than refraining from sex or heeding a list of don'ts. It is a positive, passionate existence that frees us to experience all God made us to enjoy. This is not a decision a parent can make for their child, but one they can help by walking alongside their child in a positive way. Suggested Age: 12 or 13
- **Rite of Passage:** A time to give a vision for adulthood. This can be an event or designated stretch of time to affirm and help your child anticipate and prepare for God's plan for the future in such areas like being a spouse, parent, employee, etc. Suggested Age: 15 or 16
- **Launch:** Release your child to embrace independence and intentionally launch them into a God-honoring life. A time for coaching, giving a vision for marriage and family, and preparing them for the future. Suggested Age: 17 or 18

Adoption of these disciplines and spiritual milestones has to have priority on our families calendars, otherwise, even with the best of intentions, it is most likely not going to happen. Parents need a strategy that has a catalytic system to introduce and remind parents to be intentional at certain ages and stages. Mile-markers such as birthdates and other significant milestones can serve as these markers. If we can utilize these certain times in coordination with the home, we make it easier and much more likely for our parents to follow through in making disciples. The daily tasks and to-do lists will crowd out and trump all intentionality. We need to help them get it on their calendar, or it possibly will not happen.

Measuring the New Norm

The church must cast vision and let parents know that God's plan is for them to be the primary disciple-makers, but to have the most significant impact would be to not only give parents a plan but to give them specific training and information to carry out that plan. Parents need real-life tools for these steps of faith. We must provide practical how-to's and set up the parents to win. We have to make it easy and we have to make it more likely. We also need to resource the parents by becoming knowledge brokers—helping sift through the plethora of resources. A lack of resources is not the problem. The problem is there are too many resources and not all of those resources have been created equally. Since there are more resources on healthy biblical parenting today than ever before, we have try to make it less overwhelming to parents by giving them workable material.

In the time where parenting is becoming more complex, the church must respond to the new challenges. Remind parents they have the Bible as a guide and the church is here as a partner. With all the influences—God has provided the church to be support for the parent, not the reverse. God is doing what He has always done, using the Bible, the Holy Spirit, and the church to help parents be more successful.

If we want our children to have a faith that is "impressed on their hearts" as Deuteronomy 6 depicts, the church must reestablish the home as the primary place where faith is nurtured, by training and equipping parents. It must be modeled by those of us who lead in our own families. Whatever you do as a church leader, do something! And start with your own family. We cannot pass something to those we lead unless we are practicing it ourselves.

As a church leader, we need to evaluate and measure the progress and effectiveness of our strategy to equip our parents in being the primary disciple makers.

The following is a sample list to evaluate progress:

- What is our path or strategy to equip parents?
- What types of resources and teaching are we providing to equip our parents for each spiritual discipline or milestone?
- How often are parents receiving training and resources to connect at home? Are they utilitzing the resources given? (Example—If you give kits for each step, how many are being picked up, mailed, or downloaded?)
- Do we see the culture changing? How is the impact measurable? Where do we see more parental involvement in spiritual pathways? (Example—Salvation stories begin shifting from events at church to at home with parents.)
- How are our parents passing faith and having faith discussions with their children?
- In what ways do our parents feel supported by the church in faith formation?

Consider doing a prelaunch survey/evaluation to get a baseline to measure progress. Ask a set of questions to gauge how well parents feel the church is helping to support and train them. Also ask a set of questions asking parents how confident they feel in having faith discussions and discipling their child. Then, do that same survey/ evaluation one year later. Consider doing this survey on an annual or bi-annual basis to continue to assess positive progression.

Summary

The church has to partner with parents. We need to let them take the lead and church leaders/teachers must take a support role. Set up parents to succeed. The home has always been God's plan, it still is, and it will always be. Let me pause here and say that as Christian leaders, we have to begin this whole process by bathing it in prayer. I know this seems like the "church" answer, but it really is. You have to approach the throne and call on a big God who can do big things. He created the family and desires for families to grow and be healthy. Cry out to the God who does miracles, who equips, and who gives power to parents. Ask Him to give you wisdom as you lead and then ask Him to give parents wisdom as they lead. And keep asking Him, keep seeking Him on behalf of your family and the families that you have been entrusted with. Don't miss this vital piece and just skip to strategy and organization—get on your knees first.

- Pray
- Cast vision
- Give a clear path/strategy
- Resource parents
- Measure results
- Reinforce helps for the parents

Resources to Explore Further

Here are just a few great resources available to churches to help their parents be intentional in this faith development:

- Faith Path/HomePointe Ministry. Faith Path exists to partner with churches in helping parents as they guide their child's faith journey one step at a time. Faith Path suggests a focus on specific practices and milestones at certain ages to provide just-in-time coaching to parents as they form the faith of their children. Fourteen age-specific kits have been created from birth to age eighteen to be given to parents when the child reaches the appropriate birthday. As the child ages, new coaching kits come from the church in an effort to make it easy for parents to remain intentional. Each kit includes a training video, guide, starter ideas, and other helpful elements. Training videos include specific teaching for each step from experts and other families. Faith Path masters are available for churches to license and customize for easy integration with other HomePointe tools. For more information on the complete Faith Path strategy and HomePointe, go to drivefaithhome.org.
- *My Faith Box* by Lydia Randall. A resource for parents to guide their child's faith journey and capture spiritual growth keepsakes. *My Faith Box* includes a My Faith Book inside the box. Ideal to help you create an age-specific plan on each birthday and capture memories from special milestones; while giving you resources and ideas for how to be intentional in helping your child know, love, and follow Jesus. *My Faith Box* was initially created at Lake Pointe Church to give as a gift from the church at Parent Dedication. For more information on My Faith Box or bulk pricing for churches, go to myfaithbox.org.
- Legacy Milestones at legacymilestones.com and *The Legacy Path: Discover Intentional Spiritual Parenting* by Brian Haynes. *The Legacy Path* is meant to change the culture by moving children and grandchildren toward life God's way instead of life portrayed as right in the eyes of the world. The reader will find

many practical steps explained allowing the destination to be reached.

- *Are My Kids on Track? The 12 Emotional, Social, and Spiritual Milestones Your Child Needs to Reach* by Sissy Goff, Dave Thomas, and Melissa Trevathan.

- *Take It Home: Inspiration and Events to Help Parents Spiritually Transform Their Children* by Mark Holmen and David Teixeria seeks to help congregations develop an integrated and comprehensive approach to family ministry including a package for creating a mission, vision, and strategy for family ministry; thirteen reproducible and customizable Take-It-Home Event outlines; a DVD with compelling messages for senior pastors and Christian education leaders; and a Faith at Home interactive website. Faithathome.com.

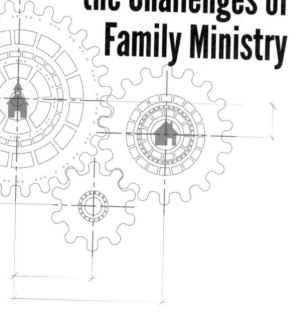

RECALIBRATE
the Challenges of
Family Ministry

10
The Picture Frames Are Different but Single Parents and Stepparents Are Families Too

Tammy G. Daughtry

Current Unhealthy Norms

For many, the "family portrait" has been broken. Shattered single parents are grasping for hope as they navigate the complexities of transition and adjustment while trying to keep their children's emotional turmoil to a minimum. The once believed dream of "happily ever after" has turned to divorce papers, parenting decrees, dividing the dishes and furniture, and only seeing their kids every other week or weekend. If there was ever a time for the church to engage and bring the true unfailing love of Christ to a person's life, it is as they are walking the road of divorce or stumbling through the emotional fallout the first few years after. In shame and defeat, many single parents will isolate and not engage in their normal church activities; what was once an experience of joy and family togetherness may, at times, seem to be a reminder of their failed marriage and their aloneness. Staying home on Wednesdays and Sundays may be a result of their own sadness and complete exhaustion of the transitions happening in their lives. We cannot assume single parents are pulling away from the church; what they are struggling with is their loss of identity as a family, the predictability of the rhythm of life they had with their spouse, and trying to "explain" what is happening to people who may not always be kind. They are in emotional shock sometimes to the point of being paralyzed to make decisions, let alone make their bed, and get to church.

Oh to be the spiritual salve to the single parent soul; to come alongside and offer a cup of cold water in the hot and dry desert land of divorce. God can redeem and make something good out of what was broken. There is still great value in each parent and child and, quite often, the parents will need outside eyes to help them continue to see their own value.

Blind Spots. Even wonderful churches have blind spots. The blind spot could be they do not recognize the extended stress and inconsistent schedule a teen has to encounter when parents are in two different locations and that getting parents to sign off on camp forms and pay deposits on time can be very difficult. A child in a single parent family may need extra financial support to be able to attend camp at all. Inconsistent attendance in Sunday School or extra-curricular church activities (choir, youth group, serving) might be specifically due to the child going to the "other parent's home" and simply having no way to participate.

Family functions at church most likely assume a two-parent family, thus unintentionally creating events and activities that expand the awkwardness for a single parent, if not clearly pointing out their aloneness.

Leaders may not realize that a single parent is still part of a family: now it is a *single* parent family, nevertheless a family with a leader and a parent who needs support. Simple descriptions or admonishment from the pulpit can get overlooked and accidentally appear to forget the single mom and the single father on special days like Mother's Day and Father's Day.

When it comes to sermons or activities supporting marriage, some leaders honestly do not understand the differences are in a first time marriage versus a blended family marriage. The blind spot is in thinking they are the same. Often well-intended events are planned for married couples and assume that anyone who is a couple will have the same motivation to attend or are facing the same struggles.

Principles in a traditional marriage retreat may not work in step-family marriage. Sometimes step-couples feel they are failing—themselves, the church, and God. It's not working so they get caught in the trap of being marginalized and isolated by the programming that churches generally lean into when they don't know the distinct differences. There are significant relationship complications between "bios" and "steps" (both kids and parents) that simply do *not* exist in an intact family system.

In an intact family, rarely does one in the house wonder whether the other people love them or even care that they exist at all. Even an annoyed teenager can still sense an unfailing love from their parents while being grounded or disciplined; however, in a single parent family, a child quite often feels jealous of the new dating relationship their parent is enjoying because it takes time away from the parent spending time with them. In nuclear, intact families, most kids don't feel jealous of mom and dad loving each other, or mom and dad going on dates or even long weekends away; instead, they mostly gain a sense of security and calm—quite the opposite for kids in stepfamilies. Kids in stepfamilies can feel very lost and alone, forgotten and not seen, and may even begin to sabotage the adult relationship out of jealousy and fear of losing contact with their own parent.

Recalibrate to a New Norm

What if every children's pastor and youth pastor (and all the trained volunteers) had an in-depth understanding of the complications in single-parent households and stepparent households so he or she could more authentically speak to the realities the kids are living in?

What if communication with kids and families was intentional so the kids that only come to church with their single parent twice a month were still connected and known? What if volunteer leaders would be assigned to specifically disciple and pursue teens who have divided homes—maybe that would mean driving across town to grab coffee with the teen on the weeks they are at the "other home" so the on-going connection was real and relevant to their day-to-day lives?

What if a specific on-going resource was made available to kids who need scholarship support to attend camps and big ticket activities and this was done pro-actively so they did not have to ask or be embarrassed to tell their leaders they can't afford to come? What if adult Sunday School classes made a priority to ask more financially established adults to be the portal of generous compassion to be sure that no kid missed these life-changing opportunities and in the process was able to see a little "peek" at how their $200 donation changed the life of a junior higher?

SOLUTIONS—Reaching Others Who Are Different From Us. Let's begin by identifying what a single parent, stepparent, and co-parent is.

Single parents. The most common type of single parent families are divorced parents; however, don't forget the widows and widowers who lost their first spouse to death. Also, consider many adults cohabitate and then divide (but don't need to divorce) so there are many non-married (never divorced) single parents in your community. One other type of single parent is a young, unwed single mom who may be living at home with her parents or living alone with no support from her parents or the baby's father.

Stepparents. Research shows the step family is now the number one family type in America. There is also wonderful research that shows how beneficial a healthy stepfamily can be when a child has the opportunity to live in a stepfamily before they launch into young adulthood. The impact of a healthy stepfamily marriage on a child will improve their emotional development and enhance their ability to have a lifelong marriage of their own.[1]

Co-parenting. Co-parenting is when biological parents live in two separate homes and have to communicate, share time, share financial obligations, and make on-going parenting decisions. It is the essence of being in the "business of parenting," but doing so from two separate addresses. Sometimes co-parenting can mean a grandparent or another caregiver is part of the family equation as a primary caregiver, but for the purpose of this chapter we will land on it being a mother and father who are no longer in a personal relationship but maintain a parenting position in the child's life. These parents may have been married and are now divorced or were cohabitating and now have moved apart.

Next, let's look at a few points of "lingo" that are important and unique to single parent, stepparent, and co-parent dynamics:

Parenting time. This is the legal term for how much time the children spend with their father and how much with their mother, as well as when and where they transition between homes. In most cases, when a child is having "parenting time" with their mom, the mother is not legally required to have the child attend or participate in activities requested by the father and vice versa. Some co-parents are able to negotiate exceptions to this, but the most common co-parent scenarios expressed will, at a minimum, create inconsistent church attendance due to parenting time.

Attachment. John Bowlby was the first attachment theorist who identified factors related to the "lasting psychological connectedness between human beings"[2] and who also defines ways to measure attachment. In traditional families, kids and parents usually have secure attachments with one another. In single parent and stepparent families, kids and parents quite often have "competing attachments."

Competing attachments are created by having a feeling of love and loyalty to one person that creates conflict with another person. Example: A child in a single parent family loves both mom and dad; however, now mom and dad don't love each other so they become, in a sense, in conflict with their own parents because the love and attachment they used to enjoy when they were a three person home is now confused and exasperated when mom and dad live separate from one another and often maintain a hostile relationship.

Competing attachments are multiplied in a stepfamily marriage because a new wife may now be an instant stepmom to three children and quite often see the stepchildren very objectively while seeing her own biological children with a deep attachment, thus having what is called "bio fog" that inhibits her ability to be objective about her own children. In the same scenario, a father can see his own biological children more subjectively than his new stepson, with whom he has not yet formed a strong attachment. Discipline styles, parenting styles, and personality styles also play into the challenge with stepfamily marriages and can often make it almost impossible to negotiate and find a satisfying "middle ground" when making parenting decisions about the children collectively.

Family Systems. We all come from a family of origin (birth family) and carry dynamics of our childhood into our adulthood. When a couple marries they create a new system. When children are added to the marriage that is another system; they are still a couple and they are also parents so there are multiple "systems" active at all times. As parents divide and often re-couple, that changes the systems drastically and often kids get caught in the on-going anger and conflict between systems.

How do you engage with multiple family systems and types? If you want to know what the single parents and stepparents need in your community, start by enlisting a few of them to serve on your planning committees and ask them strategic questions. When you are intentional to include single parents and stepparents in your programming and planning, important considerations will be highlighted for each family type. Examples include: What is it like for a single parent or stepparent on Mother's Day and Father's Day to sit in your worship service? Do they feel recognized and appreciated or lumped into the same type of family as an intact family? What other holidays are significant for single-parent families and stepfamilies and how does that impact their children? Holidays quite often mean hurt feelings, alone time when kids are with the co-parent, and the overwhelming quiet of an empty home. Helping single and stepparents navigate the emotional and social landscape of holidays can be a wonderful way to help them feel seen and heard in your church.

Some possible ways to help these unique families:

Scholarship funds. One church created an on-going scholarship fund to help two students in the youth group who had recently lost their mother in a car accident. Imagine the stress a junior high kid might feel, knowing their family is already hurting financially because of the recent death and then they are handed a camp registration form that requires a $150 deposit? What child is going to want to present that to their grieving parent, knowing things are already very tight financially, and yet what kid would want to be left behind that weekend? These two kids never had to ask for help (which can be very embarrassing and frustrating); the youth pastor identified a specific need and found older couples in the church to fund their camp fees and activity fees for about two years right after they lost their mom, so it was never even a question or concern they would be left out or left behind. He saw the situation and activated his own request to a few people in the church that were honored and excited to see their financial support meeting a real-life need in their congregation. The single dad was floored when time and time again the youth pastor simply said, "Your kids are already signed up for camp. I just need you to sign their medical release form." What a great blessing to the father, who in his expansive grief was able to simply exhale and thank God for being seen, being known, and being supported. This simple act ministered to a specific need. The church body was caring for its own and keeping those two kids connected to the very heart of God in a time they were sinking in emotional and relational pain.

Double lunch. Consider asking a large couples class to host a "double lunch" once a month after church and invite the single parents to attend. This alleviates social awkwardness for single parents of not knowing how to connect (without it feeling like asking someone on a date), it helps financially struggling single parents to have a free blessing to eat and allows their kids to have fun together as well. Having a volunteer mentor organize and promote the monthly events is a great way to start something immediately to include and connect with single parents. This is a low cost, immediate return idea you can start next week!

Parenting conference. Consider an annual parenting conference or a getaway retreat that includes single parents, stepparents, and addresses the complex family! Bring in guest speakers to address these unique concerns or host a Saturday webinar with a few strategic leaders "live" via internet if you need to keep your costs down. Consider starting a life group that specifically meets the needs of single and/or remarried parents. There are resources that focus on one or the other family type and a few exist that can affirm and encourage *both.*

Local professionals. Connect with local counseling centers and know what local resources exist to support single parents and stepparents therapeutically. Especially find therapists that do blended family work with the entire family and who have a deep understanding of "competing attachments" in complex families. Also, for practical support for day-to-day needs, ask if the local car shop, dry cleaners, car wash, or a few restaurants would donate services on occasion when there is a true single parent crisis or as an on-going way to gain goodwill in the community. Enlist a few local family attorneys to offer free guidance to single parents who may be navigating the new legal system and simply need someone to help them understand the context of their new norm. Many won't have the means to hire attorneys on a regular basis but the church can be a wealth of knowledge by even compensating a family attorney for a few hours of his or her time to be a go-to person to help calm the fear and anxiety that legal documents often create in the stress of a single parent home. Financial planners can help in the same way; maybe consider having a workshop a few times a year designed solely for the single parent on topics related to finances, emotional health, self-care as a single parent, and even cooking meals on a budget. Many community professionals might offer a free workshop a few times a year in order to build a meaningful relationship with your congregation.

What about the kids? Kids in single parent and stepparent homes have on-going unique challenges that kids in traditional families do not:

Divided time. Because they cannot attend youth events consistently, consider enlisting youth mentors that have the time to connect with them the weeks they are having parenting time with the other parent. Maybe a digital platform could help keep them connected with texts and videos and a quick "hey buddy" from the youth pastor on the weeks they can't attend in person.

Discipline is inconsistent. Since most kids live between households that don't discipline the same way, consider sharing with your children's and youth leaders that the kids in single parent and stepparent homes may have more behavioral concerns. Having a heart of compassion for kids from hard places does not mean you forgo on-going expectations for how kids engage during classes and activities; simply put, maybe a core volunteer can be equipped and available if excessive behavior issues arise. Be intentional to handle these kids with care, understanding they have parents who are probably raising them very different every other week and they may not be at the same level of social and emotional development as their peers in traditional families.

Administration. As mentioned earlier, paperwork, camp forms, and documents can get lost between mom's house and dad's house with kids in complex families. Consider getting the email, phone number, and mailing addresses of both biological parents and add them both to all communication that goes to your students (assuming the custodial parent is in agreement with that idea). This can help with getting signatures, deposits, and feedback regarding transportation needs when both bio parents receive the info. This also communicates "we care about you" to both parents, not just the parent we see in our building each week.

Meet the parents. Youth leaders who seek to build a bridge of connection with the "other" co-parent, who does not attend the church, can gain more insight into the reality of the child's life they are influencing. This effort can even possibly bring a ray of hope to the other parent if he or she no longer attends church. Consider enlisting an older volunteer in the church that has been divorced or was a single parent themselves and see if he or she might take on the intentional engagement with the "other" parent as a way to support the children, but also to simply be an example of Christ to someone who may be angry at God or feel they have been rejected by the church. Building bridges with hurting parents reflects God's heart and can be a real-life way to offer a cup of cold water to a parent who feels they are in the desert.

Emotional compass for the children. Kids in complex families don't get to see mom and dad every night. Often their two favorite humans live in two completely separate geographical locations. These locations may be ten minutes away or ten hours apart; no matter what the drive time is, it is emotionally, physically, and relationally divided for the children. These kids have one heart, and two homes. Enlisting and equipping volunteers at every age/stage of your family ministry to express honest care and compassion for these kids will go a long way as each child grows into a high school teen. Consider creating a library of books, DVDs, articles, and digital content to help volunteers be more adequately prepared to respond to the uniqueness of kids in hard places. Helping kids know it is safe to talk to their Sunday School teacher or their camp counselor about their complicated family can give a child a powerful release to express sadness and confusion. Most kids don't feel they can talk to their own parents about these things. Research reveals the critical importance of children having at least one consistent and stable adult in their life can drastically improve their IQ, their academic success, and even their future earning potential. Being seen, heard, and understood is critical for kids and it is a real way to connect when you enlist well-seasoned and prepared volunteers to know the emotional landscape these kids live in on a daily basis. College students who are mature and may have come from a complex family of their own are also a good source of volunteers who can be put in place to understand the emotional compass of kids in divided families.

Crafts and special gifts. If children's ministry or youth group is accustomed to having kids make a special item for Mother's Day and Father's Day, consider allowing the kids who also have a stepparent to make two items. Many kids live full-time with a stepparent and it can be very confusing for them on what to do with their special "Father's Day" picture or craft when their father is two states away. Children's and youth leadership who create intentional database information can know ahead of those holidays how to plan and can be part of the on-going solution so kids don't feel bad when they come home with only one item and have a stepdad or stepmom that was forgotten.

Death of a parent. When a child has lost a parent in death, the layers of grief are complicated and will never go away. Future milestones will often trigger the child to re-grieve the loss and it is imperative that leaders who work with grieving kids have training and compassion in how to help children in these times of need. Developmental stages are different for children who have a parent die when they are a toddler, school age, tween, teen, or young adult. Intentional understanding can become a great blessing to children in any area of the church, from the nursery to college age. Death does not just remove the parent from their lives; it completely reorganizes their emotional experience at every single stage of life. Though invisible to the eye, this is a very real, deep pain that grieving kids carry for their lifetime. Their new family portrait may have their stepparent standing strong beside them, but in their hearts and minds they always continue to grieve their deceased parents. An important thing to add to the information database about kids in complex families is the day their parent died as well as the deceased parent's birthday. These are emotional reminders every year for kids. Children's, youth pastors, and volunteers who want to be tuned-in to them as individuals, find out when those significant days are and consider sending a card, a note, a text, or even asking teens to have coffee or take a walk at the park to help them navigate those calendar days. Mother's Day and Father's Day are also reminders to these children of their missing parent. Being compassionate and considerate to their unique circumstances will make a meaningful difference to the child or teen.

Kids' committee or advisory council of teens. Kids in single parent and stepparent homes could give helpful feedback to leaders who are planning and preparing for future activities. A kids' committee could give some interesting insights to curious leaders who truly have not lived in or are raising a complex family like a single parent or stepparent family. Allowing kids to have a voice is genius and could lead to more effective ministry!

No more blind spots. Youth oriented events and programming that acknowledge and understand the complexities of kids in single parent and stepparent homes are needed across the country. Marriage retreats and parenting conferences for single and stepparent families are invaluable!

Weekly Sunday School classes or life groups that uniquely focus on single parenting, step parenting, or dating as a single parent can immediately express to your community that these family systems are important and unique. Having a balance of these options, along with your on-going traditional options, gives complex families a choice: some will very much appreciate having an opportunity to be together in similar life experiences and with people who "get it!" and some will choose to integrate into traditional groups. By offering a choice, you are expressing an important message to complex families: "You matter. We see you. We honor your unique experiences. You are welcome here."

Creating a flier that gives contact info and on-going classes or life group information on the menu of topics can be placed at local libraries, coffee shops, workout facilities, restaurants, and drycleaners. Social media is a powerful way to share this information as well. It's not just about an event or a conference, but it is the on-going, intentional way the leadership markets to the demographic of single parents, stepparents, and also never married parents that will catch the attention of that audience and prayerfully invite them in. Easter egg hunts and trunk-or-treat events are a great time to highlight the on-going activities for single parents and stepparents. Creating a

30-second radio spot to wish all the single moms and step moms a "Happy Mother's Day" and being sure to run it the 30-40 days prior to Mother's Day will definitely capture an audience. The same is true for fathers. They are within arm's reach of your church and quite often they are just waiting for a simple invitation.

For Valentine's Day consider a radio, social media, and even TV campaign to speak to stepparent couples and invite them to enjoy a weekend that celebrates love and stepfamily. Friday night could be a romantic dinner for step couples, hosted by your church. Provide childcare and fun activities for the kids. Treat step couples to a nice dinner at your church with a guest speaker and music by other step couples with an invitation to participate in an upcoming stepfamily life-group that will be led by another step couple in the church. A catchy radio campaign that speaks to their unique family type will perk the interest of many couples who simply stay home because their lives are busy and their family is complicated. Get in the complication with them! When you draw in the stepmoms and the stepdads you gain their trust and connection, then it opens the opportunity for kids to come along as well.

Measuring the New Norm

Be Intentional. Think Strategic!

- Of the church's services, programs, and events, how many are specifically targeting a single parent / co-parent demographic? How many target stepparents?
- What percentage of the staff are trained in family systems?
- What percentage of our church leadership, paid or volunteer, specifically focuses on family needs, and what percentage of those family ministers express a passion for and understanding of the unique dynamics of single / co-parent / step parenting?

- Does the church board, planning council, or family ministry committees intentionally recruit single parents or stepparents?
- How many single or stepparents are on the church staff?
- How many single or stepparents have a role on the platform or the worship team?
- How many single parents or stepparents are leading life groups or Sunday School?
- Does the church's budget reflect on-going strategic efforts to reach and support single and stepparent families?
- Are children in single parent homes attending retreats, summer camps, VBS, and all the other student events? (Have a plan to help with transportation as well as finances.)
- How much has been given through the financial portal to help a single parent and his or her children attend and participate in broader church activities?
- How many college students are mentoring younger students and pursing a connection with the student during the off week?
- How many grandparents are actively connecting with single parents and their kids?
- How many single parents and stepparents were involved in outreach the last 12 months?
- How many step couples are mentoring other step couples?
- How many single parents are mentoring single parents outside the church walls?
- How many people attended the annual "National Stepfamily Celebration" on National Stepfamily Day (September 16)?
- How many people attended the annual "National Single Parent Celebration" on National Single Parent Day (March 21)?*
- How many single and stepparents are there in your congregation?
- How many children are represented by those parents?

- How many surveys were given and what percentage of response are you getting from single and stepparents?

SUMMARY AND RESOURCES

In summary, we uphold the intact family but not at the exclusion of other family portraits. With the stepfamily being the number one family type in America and over 55% of children being raised in non-traditional families, expand the types of picture frames that are celebrated in your congregation.

What the church does to walk well with single parents and broken families matters! Generations to come will be impacted and healed by the consistent and intentional love and engagement with these hurting families. Little boys and girls can grow up to be godly men and women who are Kingdom-minded influencers for Christ! You can break the repetitive cycle of divorce in your community by supporting and loving complex families today.

Here is a little "peek ahead" of what the potential fruit can become a few decades later as the baby pictures fade, the graduation tassels are moved, and children in single parent and stepparent families create their own future families…your church might be raising the next Dr. John Trent!

Dr. John Trent, professor, counselor, author, and the Gary D. Chapman chair of Marriage and Family Ministry at Moody Bible Institute is from a broken home. His dad walked out when he was two and he never met him until he was an adult. Dr. Trent is now a national advocate on healthy marriage and he attributes much of this to the fact that his single mom never spoke negatively of his dad (though she had a long list of reasons she could have) and she always pointed John to God's plan for life-long marriage. As an adult, he has published forty plus books on family and marriage. Dr. Trent is from a broken home but did not have a broken life! He is a living testimony to the power of forgiveness, the choice to speak life, and the consistent decision for a single mom to stay well-connected to godly friends and a church body that loved her well! Broken homes can become loving, stable homes where kids and parents honor God and continue to see good fruit in the decades to come. The picture frames *are* different, and the church is a critical part of the lifelong outcome of raising godly kids into Kingdom-minded fathers, mothers, and future pastors and leaders.

Resources to Consider Adding to Your Church Library

- *One Heart, Two Homes: Co-parenting Kids of Divorce to a Positive Future* by Jay and Tammy Daughtry is a digital resource including 33 guests that can be used for a 10-week small group, workshops, or individual one-on-one ministry by Co-Parenting International. CoParentingInternational.com.
- *Divorce Care*, a 13-week small group study. DivorceCare.org.
- *The Smart Stepfamily*, an 8 session guide by Ron Deal. SmartStepfamilies.com.
- Solo Parent Society has many resources for single parents with leadership curriculum to lead the way. SoloParentSociety.com.

Books to Consider Adding to Your Church Library

- *Becoming a Stepkid…* by Jay and Tammy Daughtry
- *Co-Parenting Works! Helping Your Children Thrive after Divorce* by Tammy Daughtry
- *Going Solo: Hope and Healing for the Single Mom or Dad* by Robert Beeson & Robert Noland
- *My Single Mom Life: Stories and Practical Lessons for Your Journey* by Angela Thomas
- *The Smart Stepfamily* by Ron Deal

- *One Heart, Two Homes: Understanding My Divided Family for Toddlers* by Jay and Tammy Daughtry
- *One Heart, Two Homes: Understanding My Divided Family for Grade School Kids* by Jay and Tammy Daughtry
- *One Heart, Two Homes: Understanding My Divided Family for Teens* by Jay and Tammy Daughtry
- *When Dinosaurs Divorce* by Brown & Brown

WEBSITES

- CoParentingInternational.com
- CovenantEyes.com
- FamiliesManagingMedia.com
- FamilyLife.com
- FatherhoodComission.com
- Fathers.com
- ModernFamilyDynamics.com
- SingleparentSociety.com
- SisterhoodOfStepmoms.com
- SmartStepfamilies.com
- The StepmomConnection.com

Endnotes

[1] Tianyi Yu & Francesca Adler-Baeder PhD (2007), The Intergenerational Transmission of Relationship Quality, Journal of Divorce & Remarriage, 47:3-4, 87-102, DOI: 10.1300/J087v47n03_05.

[2] Andrew B. Starky BD (1999), A Theological Application of John Bowlby's Psychoanalytic Theories of Attachment, American Journal of Pastoral Counseling, 2:1, 15-47, DOI: 10.1300/J062v02n01_03.

11
When Churched Kids Don't Have Churched Parents

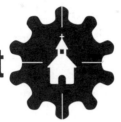

Timothy Paul Jones

The first time anyone suggested an emphasis on family ministry to me was nearly twenty years ago. I was serving as the associate pastor of a mid-sized church in a low-income neighborhood near Tulsa, Oklahoma. The person who encouraged me to consider family ministry was the new student pastor.

My first response was to reject family ministry as a preposterous idea for our context. The primary reason that family ministry seemed impossible to me was because at least two-thirds of the children and students in our ministries were kids who came to church without their parents. How could we possibly pursue family ministry when most of the participants in our ministries arrived at activities without their families?

"I really like what you're describing," I told the student pastor. "And that's probably the way youth ministry *should* be done. But it's just not possible here. Most of the students come from broken homes, and their parents are never going to come to church."

As I reflected on the student pastor's recommendations, I concluded that, if God ever called me to serve in an upper-income suburban church, I might consider focusing on family ministry—but not here. Not in this low-income exurban neighborhood, blighted with methamphetamine labs and a rundown trailer park. Not in this congregation that served children and youth whose parents would never consider becoming part of our church. Not in this place where I didn't even know most of the kids' parents.

Two years later, the church's context had not changed, but my role had. The previous senior pastor had retired, and I ended up transitioning into his position. Looking at the church from this new angle, I grew concerned as I saw fault lines emerging between generations. What's more, the children's and student ministries were growing rapidly, but it was becoming increasingly difficult for staff and volunteers to remain engaged with so many new faces. Even though the student ministry was growing in numbers, there seemed to be little—if any—multiplication in spiritual maturity.

A lot of factors came together for me that year. One of them was a renewed recognition that—no matter how difficult family ministry might be in my context—God had designed the family to make disciples and we as church leaders needed to equip parents to disciple the next generation. Another factor had to do with the absolute necessity of linking people together across the generations. I also had to admit that aiming our efforts at students and children had produced strong numeric growth in these ministries but that almost all of these students were disconnected from the church as a whole.

Little by little, in response to these recognitions, I began taking my first steps toward family ministry. At the time, I had never heard of any larger movement toward family ministry—it would be five years before the first D6 Conference took place. My goal wasn't to be trendy or cutting-edge; I was simply desperate to draw the generations together and to see children and students discipled well.

But I still had to face the same difficult dilemma that had caused me to dismiss the practice of family ministry two years earlier: *What about the students and children whose parents don't come to church at all?* This type of student still comprised the majority of youth and children in my church. And so, I began experimenting with ways to reach these children and their parents.

After nearly twenty years, I'm still experimenting.

Today, I'm a professor of family ministry as well as a pastor serving in student ministry in an inner-city church, and I'm still looking for the best ways to reach children who come to church without their parents. Along the way, I have learned much that I will share with you in this chapter—but I am not writing this chapter from the end of a journey in which I have solved this dilemma once and for all. I am a fellow traveler on this journey with you, and I have racked up far more failures than successes along the way.

Almost every week, you'll find me playing guitar in the worship band in our student ministry, mentoring volunteers, or teaching the Bible to middle schoolers and high schoolers. I'm nearly fifty years old and I've now done this for decades, but there are still nights when I wonder if I'm getting it right. Nevertheless, there have been a few practices that I've seen implemented along the way that have been remarkably effective. These are the practices that I will be unpacking in this chapter—but, before I unpack the practices, I want to take a quick look at a couple of unhealthy norms that have marked children's and students ministries for far too long.

Current Unhealthy Norms

Ministry that fits the ideal but ignores the real. In the beginning, God formed the first family by crafting the man from the dust and then providing him with a wife. God created this first couple to live in communion with Him. Then, He commanded them to multiply this fellowship by expanding their family: "Be fruitful, multiply, fill the earth and subdue it" (Genesis 1:28, CSB). Throughout this narrative, God's ideal for the structure of families is clear: a father and a mother living in fellowship with God and raising children in the context of this relationship.

Because this is God's ideal vision for families, some churches—whether intentionally or unintentionally—focus most of their efforts on families that fit this ideal. The problem is that, from the moment of humanity's fall into sin to this very day, many families don't fit neatly within this ideal. You are called to serve in a world filled with families fractured by the fall. You know this, but it's still easy sometimes to slip into patterns that focus only on families that fit the ideal. Here are a few symptoms of this pattern that I've observed over the past few years:

- The church has intergenerational worship services—but no plan for helping children who lack parental guidance to be able to engage meaningfully in these services. Unruly children are frequently the object of stares and glares from long-time members of the church.
- The church has activities that bring together children with fathers and mothers—but little or no provision is made for children in single-parent households, households that have been broken by divorce, or households where one or both parents are incarcerated.
- The church has rites of passage that are celebrated with parents to mark a child's movement toward maturity through meaningful milestones—but no plans are made for including children whose parents don't attend church.
- The church has dinners for the entire church—but little thought is given when it comes to including children who show up without parents. The same church members who stare and glare at unruly children in worship services do the same when these children pile their plates too high or act inappropriately

at church dinners. Some members may even suggest having the meals at times when only churched families will show up.

These aren't the only symptoms, of course. But, hopefully, they're enough to help you to see that, if your church has ministries that work for ideal families but not for children from fractured or unchurched families, you're probably appealing to the ideal but ignoring the real. Such churches tend to attract families with a believing mom and a believing dad in every household and no recent visits from the Department of Human Services; in the process, these churches have focused so much on the ideal that they've lost sight of the reality of broken homes and unbelieving parents.

But there's an opposite norm that's every bit as unhealthy for a church's mission. In this unhealthy norm, ministries appeal so much to what's "real" that they lose sight of the "ideal."

Ministry that appeals to the real but ignores the ideal. "Well, at least we're reaching the children!" That's the declaration I've heard over and over from church leaders whose ministries are packed with children from unchurched families.

This sentiment is not entirely wrong. After all, if a church is reaching students and children, that means the gospel is transforming the lives of young people, and that's always a reason to rejoice! But this sentiment can sometimes be symptomatic of an unhealthy norm. Whenever I hear a youth or children's minister make this statement, I try to respond with a couple of questions: "What specifically are you doing to reach these students' parents?" and "How many of these students' parents do you know personally?" What the answers to these questions frequently reveal is a ministry that has settled for reaching young people but has given up on touching the lives of their parents.

So what's the problem with this pattern? In the first place, your ministry will be less effective if you aren't pursuing a relationship with parents. Your ministry will be enriched if you know parents and they know you, even if those parents never show up in your church building. But there's a deeper and more significant problem as well: if you settle for the assumption that these parents will never become believers or members of your church, you're living as if there are limits on God's capacity to transform any heart. But there is no one who stands past the potential reach of God's transforming grace! There is power in the gospel of Jesus Christ to transform the heart of anyone who believes, and no one is beyond the reach of this grace (Romans 1:16).

Part of what I want to cultivate in you through this chapter is a gospel-centered expectancy that views every parent—no matter how broken or far from God they may seem—as a potential recipient of the gospel of grace. Never settle for the reality that some of the students in your ministry will never have believing parents. When you do, you've chosen the "real" and missed the "ideal." In the process, you lose sight of the glorious truth that no parent of any child in your ministry stands beyond the reach of the gospel of God's grace.

Recalibrate to a New Norm

Gospel-centered ministry with children and students refuses to choose between the ideal and the real. When you pursue the ideal and the real simultaneously, you'll find yourself constantly seeking opportunities to share the gospel with these parents, because you yearn for them to experience God's ideal. At the same time, because you're deeply aware of the painful reality that these parents may never respond to the gospel, you will also try to find ways to enfold their children in the church's fellowship, even if the parents never come to faith at all. This simultaneous pursuit of the real and the ideal is the new norm to develop in your ministry.

This new norm isn't easy, but it's right. What's more, this new norm never happens quickly. It's not a program that you can implement in a few weeks. It's a process of recalibration that will require years of patience and persistence. With those recognitions in mind, here are three simple recalibrations to put into place to bridge the gap between the real and the ideal when churched kids have unchurched parents.

Recognize the reality of spiritual orphans by developing families-in-faith. Care for orphans is an essential outworking of our identity in Jesus Christ. Believers in Jesus Christ are all ex-orphans adopted by God's grace. That's why James—the son of Joseph and Mary whose half-brother Jesus had been adopted by Joseph—declared that "undefiled religion" calls God's children to act on behalf of "orphans and widows in their distress" (James 1:27). In light of this calling to care for orphans, what about "spiritual orphans"—children whose parents aren't yet believers in Jesus Christ? The answer is simple: The gospel compels Christians around them to become their spiritual family.

But how—specifically and practically—can you provide families for spiritual orphans in your church?

One way that can happen is by developing a families-in-faith ministry. A *family-in-faith* is a faithful family in your church that's connected with one or more specific students or children who attend church without their parents. This is one of many key areas where senior adults and couples without children as well as parents whose kids are friends with kids of unchurched parents can make vital contributions to family ministry. Family-in-faith ministry begins as an attitude of care for spiritual orphans, but it doesn't end there. It develops from an attitude of care into a system that assigns specific students or children to specific families-in-faith. In one sense, you might think of families-in-faith as spiritual foster parents. The primary responsibility of a family-in-faith is simply to function as a family at church for the students or children assigned to them.

What this means at a very practical level is that, when a family-in-faith sees their assigned student or child walk into the sanctuary, they invite the student or child to sit with them. It means that, when there's a milestone celebration of a particular moment in the child's life, the family-in-faith is present to support the child. If the parents from the child's household don't make an appearance, the child isn't embarrassed because their family-in-faith stands as their family in the church. If the child's household parents do show up for the celebration, all the better! When that happens, the family-in-faith participates alongside the unchurched parents. At church dinners, kids whose parents aren't present eat with their families-in-faith. Families-in-faith may even meet with students or children outside of church, in public locations so there is no hint of any inappropriate relationships at any level.

Whenever I suggest that churches work to cultivate families-in-faith throughout their ministries, there are a couple of specific questions that typically come up. One of the questions is, "Why do we need to assign specific children to specific families-in-faith?" The other one has more to do with practical implementation: "How can we possibly find enough families to assign every child or student to a family-in-faith?"

The first question comes about because of my insistence on assigning specific students and children to each family-in-faith. Here's why I insist on specific kids for each family-in-faith: *specificity produces responsibility.* If you urge everybody in the church to live as a family-in-faith without connecting specific families to specific children, a few people will try their best to do what you ask. Most families in your church will, however, assume that someone else is pursuing this task. Tasks that are assigned to everyone are typically accomplished by no one. If two or three specific children are assigned to each family-in-faith, those families are far more likely to maintain strong connections with these students and children.

The answer to the second question—"How can we possibly find enough families to assign every child or student to a family-in-faith?"—requires a recognition that any change worth making takes time. In many churches, it would be impossible to find enough families-in-faith to connect them with every single child whose parents don't attend church, at least at first. There are simply too many children in proportion to the number of faithful families. If that lopsided proportion describes your church, how do you move toward a family-in-faith ministry? *You do it one grade at a time.*

Designate one specific grade as the time when you'll connect children with a family-in-faith. One year, provide families-in-faith for every child in that grade. The next year, do the same thing again with that same grade, and keep repeating this pattern until every child in that grade and older has a family-in-faith.

Here's how this might work in student ministry: You might choose sixth grade as your first family-in-faith year. A family-in-faith would be assigned to every student whose parents don't attend church when those students become sixth-graders. The year after that, those same families-in faith-would continue to be responsible for these sixth-graders when they become seventh-graders, and new families-in-faith would be enlisted for the new cohort of sixth-graders. This way, you only need to gather enough families-in-faith each year to shepherd the incoming sixth-graders and any new students that have started attending in later grades. Over the span of six years, every one of your students whose parents don't attend church would gain a family-in-faith. In children's ministry, you could start a similar system beginning with first-graders.

Developing a families-in-faith ministry takes time, but it's one of the best methods that I've seen when it comes to keeping spiritual orphans connected to the church. Even if you don't follow the precise path that I've described here, don't overlook your church's responsibility to become a family for spiritual orphans. If any family ministry fails to care for spiritual orphans, such ministry is not family ministry at all; it is idolatry of an idealized image of the family. And idolatry of family is no less despicable in God's sight than the Asherah poles of Iron Age Israel or the pantheon of ancient Rome. Families-in-faith can be one of your church's most potent defenses against slipping into idolatry of the ideal family. Select families-in-faith carefully, train them well, and provide clear expectations for their role in children's lives. Perhaps most important, celebrate these volunteers' contributions as frequently as possible.

Pursue the ideal through monthly expressions of gratitude for unchurched parents. One of the most problematic patterns in ministries that have given up on reaching unchurched parents is you may not even know the parents of the kids in your ministry. As a result, you're missing a chance to build relationships that could result in opportunities to share the gospel. One of the most effective methods that I've deployed to build these relationships is simply to call the unchurched parents once a month—but what your leaders and volunteers *don't* say on the telephone is every bit as important as what they *do* say. Don't make the parents feel guilty because they don't attend church; these parents probably already know your perspective on church attendance. Don't use this opportunity to critique their child's behavior; if those discussions need to happen, set up face-to-face meetings for that purpose. Instead, equip your leaders and volunteers to follow a simple four-step script:

- My name is ___, and I wanted to let you know how thankful I am for your child.
- We pray for your child every week. Are there any particular prayers that you'd want us to pray for your child?

- Are there any particular prayers that you'd want us to pray for your family?
- Thank you so much for letting your child be part of this ministry! We really appreciate you.

In many instances, you'll end up leaving a message instead of speaking to the parents directly—and there's nothing wrong with that. The point is to remind the parents that you appreciate them and to make certain they have an opportunity to let the church know their needs. If your leaders and volunteers begin making monthly calls of this sort, it won't take long until you begin to build relationships with a few parents that will result in better connections with their children.

Pursue the ideal through a yearly opportunity to share a meal with every unchurched parent. The final recalibration that I'm suggesting is simply to create an opportunity to share a meal at least once each year with every unchurched parent.

In a smaller church, you may be able to do this by inviting parents to share a barbecue in your backyard or by asking if you can stop by their house. One way that I've implemented this plan in a smaller congregation is by asking if I can visit with them about what the youth group will be doing in the upcoming year and then by offering to have pizza delivered to their home to feed their family while I'm there. However your church chooses to pursue this ideal, never stop seeking opportunities to share the gospel with these parents.

In larger churches, these opportunities may look more like a yearly event in the gymnasium in which the entire church provides food for these parents during an event for their kids. Round tables are set up and at least one or two volunteers from the youth or children's ministry are placed at every table. In some churches, all parents—both churched and unchurched—are invited to this parent appreciation dinner. Other churches have found that it works better to focus solely on unchurched parents, to provide them with an unexpected expression of appreciation. Either way, plan the event well, celebrate the parents with gifts and prizes, be certain that every aspect of the event overflows with gratitude, and include a clear presentation of the gospel.

Will every unchurched parent participate in these opportunities? Of course not! But some of them will, and those parents will know where to turn whenever they face a challenge that God uses to awaken their hearts to the gospel.

These recalibrations are not flashy or fast; they are incremental and mundane. I do not pretend that following these recommendations will provide a quick or easy solution to the challenge of working with students and children whose parents don't attend church. That's primarily because I do not believe there are any quick or easy solutions to this challenge, and flashy solutions are rarely lasting solutions. Lasting transformation happens through tiny actions repeated over years and decades, not through massive shifts that happen in months or moments. The most difficult aspect of implementing these recalibrations is simply staying focused on the same commitments for the long term.

Measuring the New Norm

So how will you know whether or not you're moving toward a new norm of healthy ministry to children with unchurched parents? Here are three simple benchmarks that may be helpful as your ministry grows:

Measure monthly with your ministry leaders and volunteers. How many conversations did we have this month with unchurched parents? Was this more than last month? What is the average number of monthly conversations thus far this year?

Measure yearly with your ministry leaders and volunteers. What percentage of kids in our ministry from unchurched families have been assigned a family-in-faith? Is this an improvement over last year?

Measure yearly with your entire church. What is the total number of unchurched parents who attended any event where they heard the gospel in the past year? Is this an improvement over last year?

Summary

Some ministries recognize God's ideal for the family of a father and a mother living in fellowship with God and raising children in the context of this relationship—but they overlook the reality of broken families and unchurched parents. Other ministries enter into the nitty-gritty realities of students and children, but they never try to reach unchurched parents to guide them toward God's ideal. But healthy ministry with students and children can't choose between the real and the ideal! Healthy ministry leaders are willing to recalibrate their ministries and their measures to recognize both the realities of unchurched parents and the ideal of gospel-centered households.

When churched kids don't have churched parents, your church can serve these children and their families by developing families-in-faith and by expressing gratitude to unchurched parents. Ultimately, the goal is to provide opportunities for unbelieving parents to hear the gospel of Jesus Christ, perhaps in the context of a meal together. Some of the ways you can measure your movement toward healthier ministry is by counting monthly conversations with unchurched parents, by keeping track of the percentage of kids who now have a family-in-faith, and by sharing with your church the number of unchurched parents who participated in events where they heard the gospel each year.

Resources to Explore Further

If God is leading you to pursue this pathway in your ministry, here are a few resources that you may find helpful:

- *Family-Based Youth Ministry* by Mark DeVries. This classic youth ministry book presents ways to connect students with believing adults across the generations in your church.
- *Family Ministry Field Guide* by Timothy Paul Jones. *Family Ministry Field Guide* introduces the concept of "families-in-faith" and situates this practice in a theological framework.
- *Practical Family Ministry* by editors John David Trentham and Timothy Paul Jones. *Practical Family Ministry* is packed with ideas for family ministry and includes recommendations for how senior adults can be deployed as families-in-faith.

12
Ordinary Parents, Extraordinary Father: Surviving the Prodigal Years

Christopher Yuan

When I was young, my family attended a Christian family camp every summer…even though we weren't Christians. Our lack of personal faith in Christ, however, was no mark on our reputations around camp. My brother and I, at the time, were straight-A students at school, on the high school gymnastics team (my brother was even the Illinois state champion for pommel horse), and we had both taken first place in several state piano competitions. We were textbook examples of the disciplined, respectful children that parents hoped for. And everyone at camp noticed.

In fact, one summer the camp director came up to my mother and said, "Angela, any of the kids here could grow up to become rebellious, but not yours." So who would have thought that both my brother and I—one after the other—would rebel against our family's values once we entered college?

Most of us know, or have known, a prodigal. As a matter of fact, we all were prodigals ourselves once. But no one feels the pain more than the parents of a prodigal. I know this, because my parents have survived years of waiting for me, their prodigal son.

Current Unhealthy Norm

My Prodigal Years

In 1993, I announced to my parents that I was gay. This led to massive disruption in our family, to put it lightly. At the time, my unbelieving mom rejected me. But contrary to the stereotype that Christian parents *cannot* love their gay children, it was only after she became a Christian that she knew she could do nothing other than love her gay son as God loved her—while she was still weak, while she was still a sinner, and while she was His enemy (Romans 5:6-10).

However, with no more secrets, I felt unimpeded to fully embrace "who I was." This new freedom quickly propelled me down a path of self-destruction that included promiscuity and illicit drug use. Certainly, not all gay men go down this road, but it was my reality. Ultimately, I was expelled from dental school in Louisville, moved to Atlanta, and became a supplier to drug dealers in more than a dozen states.

During this time, God graciously worked in the lives of my parents and He brought them both to a saving trust in Christ. My parents didn't realize the extent of my rebellion, but in the light of their newfound faith, they knew my biggest sin wasn't same-sex sexual behavior; my biggest sin was unbelief. What I needed more than anything else, through God's gift of grace, was faith to believe and follow Jesus.

My mother began to pray a bold prayer: "Lord, do whatever it takes to bring this prodigal son to you." She didn't pray primarily for me to come home to Chicago or to stop my rebellious behavior. Her main request was that God would draw me to Himself and that I would fall into His loving arms as His son, adopted and purchased by the blood of the Lamb.

The answer to her prayers came in an unexpected way: I was arrested for drug dealing. In jail, I experienced the darkest moments of my life when I received news that I was HIV positive. That night, as I lay in a prison cell bed, I noticed something scribbled on the metal bunk above me: "If you're bored, read Jeremiah 29:11." So I did and was intrigued by the promise I read there: "'For I know the plans I have for you,' declares the Lord, 'plans for welfare and not for evil, to give you a future and a hope'" (ESV).

I read the Bible more and more. As I did, I realized I'd placed my identity in the wrong thing. The world tells those of us with same-sex attractions that our sexuality is the core of who we are. But God's Word paints quite a different picture. Genesis 1:27 informs us that we are all created in the image of God. The apostle Paul says that in Christ "we live and move and have our being" (Acts 17:28, ESV). Thus, my identity is not gay, ex-gay, or even straight. My true identity is in Jesus Christ alone.

Initially when I started reading the Bible, I wanted to find justification for same-sex relationships. However, it was God's indwelling Holy Spirit that convicted me that trying to do so was a clear distortion of God and His Word. So I submitted to His will. I recognized that same-sex relationships were sinful and that God was calling me—and all of us—to pursue holy sexuality which is chastity in singleness or faithfulness in biblical marriage between a man and a woman.[1]

Ultimately, upon my release from jail, I committed to studying and submitting to biblical and theological truth. I enrolled in Bible college and later, seminary. Over time, God has given back the years the locusts had taken away (Joel 2:25). My parents and I now travel around the world as a two-generational ministry, communicating God's grace and God's truth on biblical sexuality.

So in light of our own brokenness and in light of the brokenness in the lives of our prodigals, how do we recalibrate the new norm?

Recalibrate to a New Norm

Breaking bad paradigms. When my parents found out about my rebellious, prodigal living, they were like most parents: at a total loss about what to do. Their own Christian faith was brand new, and they weren't sure how they should respond. But, through much counseling and prayer (much, much prayer), they realized they needed four paradigm shifts in their own ways of thinking. Here is what they learned.

First: Parents are not the cause of their children's rebellion. My mother would confess to you that, back at that family camp, when the director told her how wonderful her sons were, what she heard was, "You are really an excellent mother." So, naturally, when her sons rebelled, what she believed was, "This is all your fault." As parents of prodigals, it's important to recognize this very important truth:

It's not your fault.

You are not the main cause of your child's rebellion. Certainly, when a child rebels in a public way, it's easy for members of your church or the community to judge those parents of prodigals. And many parents carry loads of guilt—blaming themselves or their spouses for their children wandering from God.

But be encouraged! Even perfect parents have children who rebel. Take Adam and Eve, for example. They had the perfect Father and lived with Him in a perfect environment. Their Father gave them one—just one!—command, "Don't eat the fruit of the Tree of the Knowledge of Good and Evil." But just a short while later, God found His children having a snack break.

God asked Adam, "Didn't I tell you not to eat the fruit?"

"Yes," Adam replied.

"Then why did you?" (Doesn't this start to sound a little too familiar, parents?)

Adam pointed his finger right at God, "The woman you gave me, she started it!"

And round and round the blame went, until God taught Adam and Eve a lesson by allowing them to have children of their own! The pattern was set, and this cycle has never changed to this day!

If Adam and Eve gave God, in his perfect holiness, a hard time, what makes us think it will be a piece of cake for us to raise our own children? Certainly, there is always room for improvement in parenting, but we can't undo the past. Paul tells us in Philippians 3:13, "Brothers, I do not consider myself yet to have taken hold of it. But one thing I do: Forgetting what is behind and straining toward what is ahead" (Berean Study Bible).

Parents of prodigals, let go of the guilt and burden of your child's sin, and strain toward what is ahead with an attitude of possibility and hope.

Second: Parents are not the cure for their children's rebellion. My parents came to this country on graduate student visas on their own after college. With nothing, my father received two doctorates and my mother put him through both programs working a minimum wage job on the graveyard shift so she could still raise me and my brother on her own.

My parents on their own with no other help started their own successful dental practice from scratch and my mother founded and was president for a nonprofit organization that owned a multi-million dollar home for low-income senior citizens. And this was all before they came to Christ.

In their own strength, they believed and felt confident they could accomplish whatever they put their minds to. So it's no surprise this same mind-set applied when they hoped to fix the problems in my own sin life apart from God.

When first I told my unbelieving parents I was gay, my mother gave me an ultimatum: choose the family or choose homosexuality. My mother, who at the time was a typical "Tiger Mom" (a tough disciplinarian), was utterly dismayed when I didn't choose family. Instead, I packed up my bags and left. Her plan to change me didn't work, and she was devastated.

Let's contrast that, for a minute, with the father of the prodigal son in Luke 15. When the son heads off into a far country, his father does not follow him. He does not try to change his son. He does not disown his son or give him ultimatums. He does not make his son feel unwelcome at home. He never said, "I love you, but…" He doesn't say, "I told you so."

The father in Jesus's parable knows that only God can change his son, so he allowed God to work free from his own interference. He allowed him to face the consequences for his actions and to reach rock bottom. But he also waited patiently and persistently. He looked and waited for his son in the distance, and when he did finally return home, he welcomed him with open arms.

Parents, if you try to interfere and change your child's life for them, they may grow to despise and resent you. Your well-intentioned efforts may actually be hindering God's process of using consequences to turn them around. Learn from the father of the prodigal son and accept the fact that parents are not the cure for their children's sin. Only God can bring a prodigal child out of a far country.

Third: Your children are not your own. My mother will tell you, before she came to Christ, her children were *the* most important part of her life. They were more important than her work or her marriage. Motherhood was her sole identity. She did everything for us, and her life revolved around us. We were her prized possession. Or, as she now describes it, we were her idols.

But after my mother encountered Christ in a dramatic way—you can read her story in our memoir *Out of a Far Country*—she came to realize that everything she has, including her children, belongs to God. She was merely a steward of what God has given to her. God allowed her to bear and raise her children, but we ultimately belong to Him.

You've probably heard the story of Abraham and Isaac in Genesis 22. God told Abraham to take his beloved only son, Isaac, and go to the mountains of Moriah. Abraham was to sacrifice Isaac there.

This was a test of Abraham's faith. He was a very old man when God gave him his first child, and he'd waited years for him. God's promise to Abraham was tied up in this child he loved so dearly. It was the perfect condition, however, for Isaac to become an idol for Abraham. The most deceptive form of idolatry is when we worship something good. And God knew that absolutely nothing could get in the way of Abraham's relationship with God—even God's good gifts. Gifts must never come before the Giver.

Of course, when God saw Abraham's willing heart He intervened, providing a ram for sacrifice instead of Isaac. But are we willing to be like Abraham and lay our Isaac down on the altar? Could you do this? As hard as it is, we must. We can't lay our Isaacs down on the altar and then take them back! Jesus says in Matthew 10:37, "Anyone who loves his son or daughter more than me is not worthy of me" (BSB). These sobering words from Jesus are not to be taken as a divine suggestion.

My parents were faced with this difficult decision when I was sentenced to prison after being arrested for dealing drugs. My party lifestyle had gotten out of control, and now I was facing the consequences. When my mother testified in federal court on my behalf (or so I thought), her comments shocked me. "Your honor," she said, "my husband and I are not here to plead for a shorter sentence for our son. We are here to ask that our son's time in prison will be just long enough for him to turn his life to God, and no more." My mother testified in court on behalf of the Father.

Parents, if you're facing the difficult decisions involved with parenting a prodigal child, communicate clearly to them that your main goal is not their comfort or happiness, but that they would turn to God the Father who will by grace, through faith in Christ forgive, redeem, and sanctify them from their sin and rebellion.

Fourth: Love is "not enabling." Helicopter parents. Lawnmower parents. Jellyfish parents. There are so many labels for the parenting styles that are prominent today, but a desire to help children avoid any and all painful life consequences as a way of showing parental "love" is a common theme among them all. Unfortunately, many of these parents may find out later that the outcome of these short-sighted parenting decisions may lead to worse consequences than they originally feared.

Enabling is doing something with the intention to help or protect your child, but it only perpetuates the root problem. We see examples of enabling behavior when a parent defends their child's inexcusable misbehavior in class, rather than partnering with the teacher to enforce a consequence.

It's when we make excuses and point blame at other children for our child's poor decisions, or suggest that our child is being wrongly accused and is a "victim." It's finishing our child's homework for them, or calling in sick when they haven't finished work that is due. It's continually bailing our child out of jail when there has been no change of heart.

The result of enabling children is they do not learn to take responsibility for their own lives or face the consequences of their actions, nor do they become aware of their own behavior and how it impacts others. Without these consequences, they'll never identify their need to change. Simply put, enabling pushes our children farther away from God.

In 2 Samuel 13, a great tragedy happened in King David's household. Amnon, David's son, raped his half-sister Tamar. Later, Tamar's brother, Absalom, took revenge by killing Amnon. Although Amnon was guilty, Absalom did not have the right to take his life, so he fled.

What did David do? Nothing. Absolutely nothing. David, like many parents today, feared confronting his son face-to-face with his sin. He allowed Absalom to return without punishment for his sin, although he did refuse to see him. David enabled his son by not allowing him to experience the consequences of sin.

You might be thinking, "Well, my child isn't a *murderer*. It's not *that* bad." But we must understand that children must face the consequence of smaller sins in order to understand the consequences of larger sins. If they do not learn this lesson at home, they'll face many greater problems later in life.

In my college years, I'd developed a lavish lifestyle that centered around clubs, doing drugs, and flying from city to city and party to party selling drugs. Skipping school and patient appointments in the dental school clinic became the norm. Even though I already passed the national board exams, I was expelled from dental school just three months before I was to receive my doctorate.

Becoming a doctor and following in my dad's footsteps was not only my plan, but my parents' plan for me too. It would have been shameful for my parents to face their friends and family with the knowledge that I had been expelled from school. So when my parents flew down to Louisville to meet with the dean, I was confident that I'd still be able to graduate.

However, my mother had been fervently praying. She was fasting every Monday for seven years and once even fasted thirty-nine days for me. Although little change occurred in my life, God was radically changing her. She knew God's plans were greater than hers, and she needed to "let go and let God" with my life. As we sat in the dean's office, she told him, "It's not important that Christopher becomes a dentist. What's more important is that Christopher becomes a Christ follower."

To say I was shocked and angry would be an understatement, but my parents chose to get out of God's way in my life. It would be years before their prayers would be answered, but they did not get in God's way by enabling me in the name of "love."

Measuring the New Norm

Truth be told, as problematic as they were, my drug dealing and same-sex relationships weren't my biggest problems. The core issue was my unwillingness to surrender to God. In order for my parents to walk with me—or wait patiently for me—as I journeyed from the far country of rebellion into the loving arms of my Father, they needed to surrender and submit as parents, too. If you're also waiting for a prodigal, here's how to live in your new normal until they return home.

Reflect Jesus through your own brokenness. Although parents are not the cause of their children's sin and cannot cure them of their sin, they can still hope to have godly influence over their children even when they are in a far country. Start by reflecting Jesus in your weakness and in your own brokenness.

Parents must understand they are just as capable of sin as their children. Your sin may seem insignificant or harmless (whether it's pride, jealousy, gossip, slander, envy, greed, complacency, or idolizing our jobs, children, bank accounts, sports, television, and so on), but they are just as odious in God's eyes. Realizing our own brokenness in front of God will lead us to a place of humility.

When parents say, "I am sorry," to our children, it shows by example how to humble ourselves and express a teachable and moldable heart. We do not suddenly become perfect parents or a perfect family, but our children will experience parents being real with them in a deeper relationship. It will make an impact.

In Isaiah 42:3, the prophet says, "A bruised reed he will not break, and a smoldering wick he will not snuff out. In faithfulness he will bring forth justice" (NIV). God listens intently to parents who are broken and contrite (Psalm 51:17).

Reflect Jesus through your daily devotion. How would you answer these questions? Can your children see Christ in your daily life, and are they able to tell your testimony? Is your relationship with God vibrant and real? Are you a new creation, being renewed each day? Or are you pretty much the same as you were ten years ago?

And do you have a good answer for these good queries? Do your children see, without a doubt, you love the Lord with all your heart, soul, and mind? Do your children know you pray and study the Bible, even when others aren't watching? Do you show excitement and joy when you talk about God? When was the last time your children saw you share the gospel with someone else?

We shouldn't be Sunday-only Christians. Our faith should impact every day of our lives. If we want our children to take our faith seriously, then we must take it seriously too...and let it show. Studying the Bible, praying, and fasting should become part of our daily routine when God is the Master of our lives and our households.

Joshua said, "As for me and my house, we will serve the Lord." This should be a reflection of your family too, not as a forced chore but as a joy and desire. Pray for your children, with your children, and over your children.

Our relationships with Christ will never be any greater than our relationship to God's Word. Our minds need to be renewed every morning. Read Scripture, meditate on it, and challenge yourself to live it out daily.

During the years I was in deep rebellion and then in prison, my mother developed a habit of fasting every Monday in obedience to God. She developed a hunger for seeking God's face and hearing His voice. By God's grace, she once fasted 39 days, interceding for me and many others.

But fasting wasn't something she *did*. It wasn't an item she checked off her to-do list. For my mom, fasting naturally flowed out of a consistent prayer life. A consistent prayer life naturally flowed out of personal revival. Personal revival naturally flowed out of daily devotion. And daily devotion naturally flowed out of loving God and being immersed in His Word.

During those dark days of my wandering, my mother's and father's deep devotion to Christ made Christ visible to me. They lived the gospel before they preached the gospel.

Reflect Jesus through your marriage. A marriage based on biblical principles should reflect the perfect love Jesus has for his bride, the church. Your home should be a haven, a safe place that represents the love God has for his children who want to come home.

Do your children, including your prodigals, think of your home as a haven? Do they enjoy your hospitality or run from it? In my family's Chinese tradition, it's common to spend more time with family picking on one another than showing love and respect for one another.

It's rare for spouses in Chinese homes to say "I love you" in front of their children. But your children need to hear this. The more we express our love to each other, the more our children will feel free to express their love too.

In many Christian homes, it's common for parents to leave the spiritual instruction to mothers. Moms often take care of the kids' school responsibilities and are frequently the volunteers in Sunday School classes. But in Deuteronomy 6:7, God commands the fathers in Israel to teach their children to fear the Lord and live according to God's ways.

It's not only the mother's job, but the father's job to do this too. If you are the father of a prodigal child, do your children know you fear the Lord? Do you live according to His ways? Do you talk with your children about it? If not, find ways to open communication. It's okay to start small, but you must start somewhere.

Reflect Jesus through your grateful heart. First Thessalonians 5:18 tells us to give thanks in all circumstances. Not just for the good times, but also in the difficult times. For a parent, there are few more difficult times than watching your child wander aimlessly as a prodigal. But, find reasons to sing praises to God. Look to God, and focus on His promises.

On the mirror in my mother's bathroom, she has the lyrics to this hymn:

Turn your eyes upon Jesus
Look full in His wonderful face
And the things of earth will go strangely dim
In the light of His glory and grace.

As she wakes up every morning, she is reminded of where her focus must be. It must be on Jesus.

On December 8, 1998, my mother was just returning from her Bible Study Fellowship weekly training for leaders. Her heart was filled with joy after a morning of wonderful Bible teaching and fellowship. As she walked in the house, the phone rang and it was a collect call from the Atlanta City Detention Center. I had just been arrested and found myself in jail.

Her heart sank and tears began running down her cheek. But at that moment, the hymn she sang earlier that morning came to her

199

mind, "Count your blessings name them one by one." So, she tore off a small piece of adding machine tape from the calculator next to the phone and wrote down these first blessings.

Christopher is in a safe place (compared to before) *and he called home for the very first time!* Even in the midst of trials, God is still good and His blessings are still present. As my time in prison passed, she kept adding to this list of blessings. This list not only reminded my mom that God is faithful and His mercies are new every morning, but it also helped her remember not to focus on the hopelessness. Rather, she had to count God's blessings. Even in the midst of difficult circumstances, we all can still have a grateful heart.

Summary Bullet Points

Whatever your situation and trial may be with your prodigal at the moment, remember that your child's rebellious behavior is not the biggest problem. The biggest problem is your child's need to put their faith in Christ and accept God's grace to redeem and sanctify her or him.

But also know that God's love for you—and for your wandering child—is unfailing. Trust Him and focus solely on Him. Do your best to glorify Him in the midst of your trials, and look for His mercies each morning.

Remember:

- Parents are not the cause of their children's rebellion.
- Parents are not the cure of their children's rebellion.
- Your children are God's, not your own.
- Love is "not enabling."

And, instead of focusing on fixing your child, focus on:

- Reflecting Jesus in your daily life.
- Reflecting Jesus through your daily devotion.

- Reflecting Jesus through your marriage.
- Reflecting Jesus through a grateful heart.

Resources to Explore Further

Out of a Far Country: A Gay Son's Journey to God, A Broken Mother's Search for Hope by Christopher Yuan and Angela Yuan.

Holy Sexuality and the Gospel: Sex, Desire, and Relationships Shaped by God's Grand Story by Christopher Yuan.

Habits of Grace: Enjoying Jesus Through the Spiritual Disciplines by David Mathis.

Endnote

[1] Christopher Yuan, *Holy Sexuality and the Gospel: Sex, Desire, and Relationships Shaped by God's Grand Story* (Colorado Springs: Multnomah, 2019).

13
Marriage: Your First and Most Important Ministry

Scott Kedersha

Neither pastors nor ministry leaders would ever say they don't care for the marriages in their church or ministry. No effective senior pastor would get up in front of the church and devalue the importance of strong marriages. As we lead in ministry, we wouldn't stand in front of a room of leaders or in a small group huddle and say we didn't care for the marriages and families of those we lead.

Yet most churches do very little to grow healthy marriages. Outside of sending couples to professional counselors or some mandatory, ineffective, perfunctory premarital counseling, most churches don't do much of anything to grow healthy relationships.

I've never heard of a healthy church that doesn't provide children's ministry and student ministry. And I'm thankful for this! But why would we support kids and students and do very little, if anything, to strengthen their parent's marriages?

Why does this contradiction seem to exist? Why do we preach about and challenge others to grow strong marriages, yet our church does very little to support, equip, and care for couples? Something needs to change. We need to recalibrate the way we think about growing healthy marriages in the body of Christ.

Current Unhealthy Norms

The statistics differ on the actual rate, but we all know studies generally claim a divorce rate around 50% both inside and outside the church. What we don't know is the percentage of married couples who simply co-exist and tolerate one another. Regardless of the numbers, we all should believe the number is way too high. An unhealthy marriage norm exists in the marriages of the couples we lead and even in the marriages of the couples we lead with. It might even be in our own marriage.

The church can no longer idly sit by and raise its hands in frustration of not knowing what to do. We care about healthy homes and kids. It's time for the church to raise the value of marriage and healthy homes.

We must acknowledge the unhealthy norms in the marriages of ministry leaders (both staff and non-staff).

Unhealthy marriages in leadership. Many churches don't do marriage ministry because senior leadership doesn't want the microscope on their own marriage. They know what the Bible says *about* marriage, but if they talk about it in sermons or develop ministries to grow marriages, then they know all eyes might turn to their own marriage. Too many leaders sacrifice the health of their family for the needs and acclaim of ministry.

Ministry demands a lot of our time. The best and worst parts of working in ministry are all due to the fact that we work with people. It's a great calling and a major challenge. People take time and energy. Ministry leaders often sacrifice our marriage and family so we can help strengthen the marriage and families of others in our congregation or under our leadership.

Todd Wagner, the lead pastor of the church I'm a part of, often asks our staff this question: "How's your ministry?" When he asks this question, he's never asking about the size or success of a ministry event. He doesn't want to know the number of attendees or even the number of spiritual conversions. Rather, he's asking how we're doing at loving the Lord, our spouse, and our kids.

Leader: How's your ministry?

Burnout in ministry and at home. Because of the demands of ministry, many end up walking away from leadership vocationally or as lay leaders. Maybe we don't sacrifice our marriages as mentioned above, but we realize we have nothing left in the tank for our home life.

The demands of ministry often take so much time that we don't have anything left for the ones we're called to love the most. Our kids get some of our energy, but our spouse gets none. While we might not get divorced, the demands of ministry can compromise our marriage because we're not doing anything to tend to our most important human relationship. We're together but only because we either don't believe in divorce or we will lose our career.

Over the last 13 years in full-time vocational ministry, at times, I chose to serve others over my family. I'm faithful and kind to my wife and I often tell my kids I love them, but my lack of presence can communicate something different. I hate to admit it, but I've prioritized other couples, meals with leaders, writing projects, and speaking gigs over my time with Jesus and quantity and quality time with my family. By the time I get home or finish serving others, sometimes I have nothing left to give to my family. Even as a marriage pastor for 13 years, I still miss the mark here on a regular basis.

Leader: Who or what is getting your best time and attention?

The church and its leadership look hypocritical. The last few years have seen many ministry leaders fall morally. We've all heard stories of men and women in full time ministry who engage in extramarital affairs. I personally know ministry leaders who have fallen morally, and a quick glance at social media or the news will reveal many more broken ministry relationships.

If men and women leading ministries in local, healthy churches can't stay faithful to their spouse, then how do we think the world sees the church? They think we're a bunch of hypocrites who preach one thing and do another.

And this doesn't just apply to marital fidelity. Whenever we fall short (which we all do) but cover it up or pretend, everyone gets hurt in the process. Proverbs 28:13 says, "Whoever conceals their sins does not prosper, but the one who confesses and renounces them finds mercy" (NIV). When we conceal and hide our sin, we will not prosper. Rather, when we confess and forsake our sin we will be shown mercy. As a leader in ministry, we must live out our faith with authenticity and vulnerability. When we hide, no one prospers.

Leader: Are there any areas in your life where you declare one thing but do another?

If we don't help them, someone else will. We're all learning from someone or something. Google any topic and hundreds of thousands of results pop up in less than one second. One of the ways ministry has changed over the years is the availability of content to anyone, anywhere. Ministry professionals no longer corner the market on providing counsel to couples.

I can find whatever I'm looking for within seconds on TV, social media, and the internet. If the church doesn't make the effort to help marriages, then someone else will help prepare, enrich, and restore their relationships. Unless we make the decision to stand up and speak truth about marriage, then Snapchat, Saturday Night Live, and Kim Kardashian will tell men and women in our church what to believe about marriage.

Leader: We all learn from someone and something. What are you doing to equip and help couples grow in their relationship?

Our kids' most impactful picture of marriage comes from the home. I remember when my friend John showed me a picture of his four kids. We both started to tear up as he talked about the fact that someday one of his kids could end up walking away from the Lord. He wasn't planning on it, and he and his wife were doing everything they could to raise their kids to know and love Jesus. But after watching some friends of ours struggle with parenting prodigal children, we both acknowledged any one of our own kids could end up walking away from the Lord.

Our conversation challenged me to think through what my kids are learning about marriage from Kristen and me. I can't control what they think and believe, but I know they will get their most clear picture of following Jesus and loving a spouse from what they see in our home. Every day as a ministry leader, I try to strike the right balance between trusting God with the hearts of those I lead while I balance the stewardship He has entrusted to me to help model what it looks like to follow Jesus (1 Corinthians 11:1) and love my spouse (Ephesians 5:22-33). No one is watching more closely and learning more fully than our children.

Leader: What does your marriage and your view of marriage communicate to your children? Acknowledge the fact that they'll learn more from you than another other human being.

Pride affects us more than we realize. Most people I know don't want others looking in on their lives. Pride prevents us from hearing from others. We don't want others to wound or sharpen us when we fall short (Proverbs 27:6, 17). The other side of the equation is that sometimes we're all just too "nice" to each other. We should always be gentle and patient (Galatians 5:22-23), but sometimes our fear of man prevents us from sharpening one another (Galatians 1:10).

And when our pride or excessive "niceness" gets in the way, we don't grow. Part of the unhealthy norm in our marriages is that we don't play the role community is intended to play in growing our marriages. We must be willing to help each other grow by being humble and listening to an admonishment from a brother or sister in Christ. And we must be willing to wound someone we love to help them grow in their relationship with Christ and their spouse. It's not good for us to be alone, so we need to play the role God has given us to play.

Leader: Are you too proud, or do you lack the willingness to be vulnerable to listen to the counsel of others? Are you willing to help sharpen the marriages of those around you?

Recalibrate to a New Norm

Our church has become known as one of the leading voices in marriage ministry in the U.S. When we started the marriage ministry at our church, we pictured a safety net. We wanted to think through how to "catch" every category of couples: seriously dating, engaged, newly married, first-time parents, empty nesters, struggling couples, blended families, and every married couple in between. We then, systematically over the years, developed ministries and leaders to help every stage along the continuum. We didn't start everything in year one, and there are still to this day some ministries we're waiting to start. The bottom line is that we planned the steps out and did something!

Our marriage ministry strategy is to prepare nearly-weds, establish newlyweds, and enrich and restore all marriages. We do this through various discipleship ministries and through our church's small groups. It's not a perfect model, but it works for our church context. Sometimes, the hardest thing to do is to start. Start doing something to help marriages, because too much is at stake (as we saw above) to do nothing.

To be practical and helpful, the following are seven specific ways we can help the marriages in our church recalibrate to a new, healthy norm.

Help them build their home. In Matthew 7:24-27, at the end of the Sermon on the Mount, Jesus encourages His followers to build their lives on the solid rock foundation. He tells His followers storms and trials will come, and depending on where and how we build our home, we will either stand firm or wash away. We can help couples by reminding and showing them how to build their lives and marriage on the rock.

We need to disciple them: show them how to read the Word, pray together, be on mission as a couple, and share with each other what God is teaching them. Always remind them _why_ they want to be spiritually intimate with each other. We don't spend time with the Lord to check a box but to grow in our understanding of Who He is, our love for Him, and to better understand His sacrificial love for us.

How are you doing at building your home on the right foundation?

Remind them to do the things they did in the beginning. In Revelation 2:4-5, John is not writing about marriage, but he does remind the readers/listeners of the Word to do the things they did in the beginning. When a couple met each other and started dating, they did whatever they needed to do to impress their significant other. They creatively pursued them, and dated each other's PR departments. They ate healthy, worked out, and took care of themselves. They also put the needs of the other before their own, and cared for each other.

Couples then get married, move in, grow their family, pay bills, and get stuck in a rut. They lose the creativity and no longer pursue each other in exciting ways. They get bored and then years down the road either get divorced and start over again or they stay married and merely co-exist. We must remind couples to pursue each other again.

I've asked hundreds of couples about their favorite part of marriage. The overwhelming response is companionship and friendship. We develop a deep friendship when we date and then fade into becoming roommates.

Tell them to date each other. Be creative. Try something new and do something out of your comfort zone. Try to outdo each other in honoring your spouse. Do the things you did in the beginning.

When's the last time you laughed until you cried with your spouse?

Tell them life is better together. Genesis 2:18 says, "The Lord God said, 'It is not good for the man to be alone. I will make a helper suitable for him'" (NIV). We're reminded, from the beginning, that it's not good for us to be alone. God designed us with a need for others.

If we're going to help marriages in the church, we need to create ways for them to be in community with other followers of Jesus. We need people who will wound us (Proverbs 27:6), sharpen us (Proverbs 27:17), and encourage us when we need to be lifted up (Proverbs 25:11). We need others to help provide advice (Proverbs 12:15) and to help us grow wise (Proverbs 13:20). The one who rejects correction and help is stupid (Proverbs 12:1). Remind your people of the benefits of community and look for ways to help them find it.

How can you invite others into deeper relationship in your life?

Understand the goal of communication. Very few of us know how to communicate or resolve conflict. We raise our voice, argue, talk, reluctantly listen, and then talk again. Instead we need to be people who are quick to listen, slow to speak, and slow to become angry (James 1:19). The goal of conflict should be mutual understanding, not winning. Proverbs 18:2 says, "Fools find no pleasure in understanding but delight in airing their own opinions" (NIV). Don't be a fool and help your people not to be fools. Help couples communicate and resolve conflict in a way that honors God and helps grow their marriage.

Do you communicate and resolve conflict like you're on the same team or like enemies?

Fight for intimacy. When we hear the word intimacy, most people typically think primarily of physical or sexual intimacy. While this is certainly a component of intimacy, we need to expand our definition. To be intimate with someone means that we know them, are known by them, and we don't fear rejection. This is the way the Father views us in Christ: even though He knows our thoughts, actions, past, present, and future, He still knows us, desires us to know Him, and even though He knows everything about us, doesn't reject us.

Genesis 2:25 says, "Adam and his wife were both naked, and they felt no shame" (NIV). Most of us don't know how to walk through life without experiencing shame. We don't like the way we look or act and we're often obsessed with what others think about us. Genesis 2 gives us a beautiful picture of what it's like to know, be fully known, and not to fear rejection. We need to help couples fight for intimacy in marriage: spiritual, emotional, relational, and physical intimacy. The fall of man did everything it could to destroy oneness and intimacy, but we need to do all we can to help couples restore the intimacy we desire and God designed and intended.

What's one way you can be more fully known by your spouse?

Appreciate those differences: We married someone different from ourself. Thank you, Lord, for this truth! We marry someone different than ourself. We come from different families, have different personalities and unique preferences, and one of us is a male and the other a female. We're both sinners and we each think our way is better and the other is weird. We need to learn how to live with each other in an understanding way.

In 1 Peter 3:7, Peter addresses the differences between spouses. He says, "Husbands, in the same way be considerate as you live with your wives...so that nothing will hinder your prayers" (NIV). When he tells the husband to be considerate of his wife, he's telling him to live with her in an understanding way. You can also say he is instructed to live with her "according to knowledge." This means he must be a student of his wife and learn to understand her. This verse is written to the husband but the principle applies both ways. The wife should also seek to live with her husband according to knowledge, in an understanding way.

If the couples we lead are going to thrive, then we need to help them appreciate, embrace, and celebrate their differences. If we don't and they don't, then they'll drive each other crazy and their prayers will not be answered (See the last part of 1 Peter 3:7). Rather, we want to instruct and challenge our couples to do nothing that will hinder the prayers of either spouse.

Do your differences push you apart or draw you closer together?

Help each other develop the character of Christ. One of the great gifts of marriage is that every husband and wife can help the other grow to become more like Jesus Christ. The subtitle of Gary Thomas' book *Sacred Marriage* says it well: "What If God Designed Marriage to Make us Holy More Than to Make Us Happy?" You have the distinct privilege of helping your spouse develop the mind and character of Christ.

Married couples can help each other become more servant-minded (Mark 10:45). They can help each other become more humble (James 4:6; 1 Peter 5:5) and can help fight sin struggles. I love the way my wife helps me fight my gluttonous eating patterns and my struggle with lust. She bears my burdens (Galatians 6:2), and I do the same for her in her battle with people-pleasing and control. I help her process decisions to make sure she's not saying "yes" to opportunities simply so she doesn't disappoint others. I pray for her and with her in her struggles.

What can you do help your spouse become more like Jesus?

This is just a small smattering of the ways you can help the couples in your church grow their relationships and recalibrate to a new, healthy norm.

Measuring the New Norm

How can we truly measure the success of a marriage? Is it the number of kids we have? While we all know children are a blessing from the Lord (Psalm 127:4), we cannot measure success based on the number of kids in our home. Maybe it's the health and success of our children? Negative. We all know great kids who come from broken families and broken kids who come from great families. Is it our ability to resolve conflict or maintain a budget? Maybe it's the cleanliness of our home or how much money we make, give, or save? All good things, but none of the above. How about the frequency of date nights or the number of nights per week we're intimate with our spouse? No and no again.

So how do we measure success? We made the decision years ago at our church that we would not measure success based on the number of attendees at any given marriage event or by any of the metrics measured above. Rather, we decided we would measure success by *our ability to be and make disciples*. In other words, success would be evaluated by how much we looked like Jesus Christ. Full devotion is not just for senior pastors or ministry leaders. Rather, every follower of Christ is called to love the Lord with all his heart, soul, mind, and strength and to love his neighbor as himself (Matthew 22:36-40).

So what does our relationship with Christ look like? How about those in the ministries we lead? Instead of setting out with a goal of helping make great moms, dads, husbands, and wives, what if we set out to help grow disciples? What if everything we did pushed couples to become more like Jesus Christ? The men and women I know who look like Christ:

- Are in the healthiest marriages.
- Are the best parents.
- Know how to identify areas of selfishness (James 4:1) and are quick to confess and forsake sin (Proverbs 28:13).
- Put the needs of the other before themselves (Philippians 2:3-4) and serve their spouse both in and out of the bedroom (Mark 10:45; 1 Corinthians 7:3-5).
- Share together what they're learning and are humble (James 4:6). They pray with and for each other.

They do all these things not because they set out to win the husband or wife of the year award. Rather, they set their minds on things above, not on earthly things (Colossians 3:2), and became more and more like Jesus Christ every day.

Imagine what would happen in our churches if we played a part in growing healthy marriages, not by teaching couples to budget, communicate, and have great sex, but rather by helping them become more and more like Jesus Christ. That's the kind of church people want to be a part of and that's how we recalibrate marriages in our church.

Summary Points
- Couples in the church should have the healthiest and most thriving marriages around. Unfortunately this is not the case. The church needs to be the place where couples can find help in any stage of life for any reason.
- The church needs to do something to help couples. We can't sit by and miss out on the great opportunity to shepherd couples in their relationship with Christ and their marriage.

- We should seek to measure success by our ability to be and make disciples. Full devotion to the Lord is the norm for any follower of Jesus.
- Our efforts should go toward discipling people in their relationship with Christ. The hope shouldn't be to make better husbands or wives, but rather to help them grow in their love for and devotion to Jesus Christ.

Resources to Explore Further

I wrote the book *Ready or Knot? 12 Conversations Every Couple Needs to Have Before Marriage* (Baker Books, 2019) as a biblical, practical, and authentic guide to help couples prepare for marriage. The content is geared toward seriously dating, engaged, and newly married couples, but any couple would benefit from the content.

My home church, Watermark Community Church, developed a wide assortment of materials and ministries to help couples in every stage of life. We also feature a 12-step Christ-centered, biblical recovery ministry called re:generation recovery. We do training conferences throughout the year for churches who are interested in learning more about how to start or improve marriage and recovery ministry in the church. All the details for our ministries and training conferences can be found at WatermarkResources.com.

My own website has articles and resources for couples: www. scottkedersha.com.

14
Guiding Teens and Their Parents Through Cultural Challenges

Scott Turansky and Joanne Miller

"Dustin is hanging out with the wrong crowd, many of them through his online gaming. His self-confidence is low and his school performance is suffering. He believes that he's entitled to his electronics and that contributing to our family life is beneath him. How do we help him see that he's got to grow up?"

"My daughter, Jen, was caught sexting. This isn't how we raised her. She made a commitment to Christ when she was younger, but she is now consumed with fashion trends and guys. Got any ideas?"

Are parents coming to you with similar tough questions? How do you help moms and dads reach the hearts of young people in this high-energy "me first" world we live in? Developing youth ministry is like trying to hit a moving target. If you go too deep you miss the kids who need their senses dazzled in order to hold their attention. If you offer high-energy flashy programs, you may lack the depth to communicate how crucial the gospel message is to everyday life.

Furthermore, young people often flip back and forth from wanting to be entertained to feeling too grown up for childish activities. This further complicates staying relevant in their lives.

Current Unhealthy Norms

Many churches are recognizing the need to move beyond activity-driven and relationally-centered youth ministry. Those two approaches are not enough today to meet the huge demands of the adolescent challenge. In fact, sometimes youth ministry inadvertently contributes to the me-first, socially pressured world our kids live in.

Youth ministry has, in many cases, focused on relationship as an end in itself and not a means for developing disciples for Christ. Discipleship has been replaced by simply conducting activities at the church. Furthermore, the lack of coordination between home and church has weakened the impact. Parents have delegated much of the essential life training to the church and the church too often has accepted it.

Many kids today come to church to bide their time and oblige their parents. Or, if they are eager to come to church, their goal is often to spend time with their friends. If the success of youth ministry is simply measured by attendance, good times, and happy faces, then the most significant challenges are likely not being addressed.

Activity and relationship are both valuable tools, but that's exactly what they are: tools. They become vehicles for the bigger goal: communicating a sense of mission.

Young people are developing their own values and convictions. Relationship is a vehicle to impart a vision for discipleship and to communicate a sense of urgency for the adolescent years.

When youth leaders, parents, and young people share the misconception that entertainment is the goal, the result is stunted growth. Furthermore, when sports performance and participation become more important than spiritual development, imbalance robs young people of the needed nutrients that help them to manage life.

Adolescence is the stage of life's journey when young people prepare their hearts to live the adventure of adulthood in a wild and crazy world. Teenagers are on a God-given mission to understand themselves, get to know God, develop their strengths, and empower life-skills to face the challenges of living in society.

Fourteen-year-old Callie said it this way. "I feel like I'm in a race that never stops. Every time I look a different direction, there's something new. I'm continually trying to evaluate whether that idea or activity is good or bad or right or wrong, or even if it's something I'm interested in or it's just the latest trend my friends are pushing."

Callie's description is helpful. But the task is much bigger. The adolescent years are a race to build internal strength before the waves of temptation bring lasting damage. In fact, when the speed of life exceeds the heart's capacities, dangers loom.

Another mistake of both the church and the home is to equate adolescence with the teen years, ages 13-18. That idea misses the bigger opportunity. The work of growing up starts earlier than ever today. In most young people, the stage of adolescence spans from ages 10 to 25. It's during these years that many young people fail or begin a life of destructive tendencies. Teen pregnancy, crime, addiction, dropping out of school, and wrong friends are just a few of the pitfalls that dramatically alter one's life. And those big problems often start in the heart with a bad attitude, disrespect, or defiance.

When young people make wise choices, prepare well, and master certain life skills during adolescence, then their life both now and after age 25 can run more smoothly and be much more satisfying. The goal is to teach youth how to live and stay on the adventurous narrow path during adolescence. In the same way, if they get off the path, then the damage caused can leave a young person limping through life.

Furthermore, churches must embrace parents in youth ministry. The inclination to view church leaders as the experts and only work with the young people misses a huge opportunity. Parents are the primary spiritual influence in their kids' lives and they need training too. Many parents don't view the church as a place that will help them learn to teach and train their kids. Recalibration is necessary to help churches become discipleship centers to strengthen the hearts of youth and train parents to know how to equip them as well.

Recalibrate to a New Norm

So how do we get hold of the hearts of our youth? What can we do to compete with the fast-paced, highly electronic society they live in? Must we match the loud and flashy environment or can we teach young people to respond to a higher calling?

The best growth takes place when three partners work together, the young person, the parents, and the church. This strategic partnership can equip young people to accomplish the mission of adolescence. Honing down the objectives and the practical tools provides the strength needed for them to not only survive but to thrive.

You are in a strategic role and often become the leader in this partnership. Your mission must be clear as you attempt to influence young people and their parents.

Four principles can guide you as you lead the charge to help young people meet the growing demands of adulthood. These four goals will guide your programming and will help you measure the success of your ministry.

Communicate a mission-oriented view of life. It's simple. Children play. Adolescents prepare. Adults work. Most young people haven't grasped this yet. Many think they will play until adulthood, but by then, the catch up required can be overwhelming.

Adolescence is a time of preparation that puts them on a mission. Many young people fail today because of their misunderstanding of their calling. They think their goal in life is pleasure. In the end, pleasure itself doesn't produce the deep satisfaction we all need in life. Rather, it's illusive, requiring more and more of a positive sensation to get the same feeling. On the one side, this compulsion results in addiction. On the other, the lack of fulfillment has driven many young people to suicide. They just can't handle the pressure of life.

Life is not a joy ride where happiness is the goal. It's a battlefield where off-roading can hit minefields. Temptation's advertisement is pleasure. It comes in many forms. It might be the high of taking a drug, the stress relief of smoking, the feeling of being valued by a person who is interested in you for sex, the sweetness of revenge, the thrill of getting away with cheating, or the approval of peers that requires disobeying the law.

It's amazing how many young people believe their goal right now is to have fun. And, many parents encourage it! Young people often have a hard time understanding the role of pleasure in a healthy person. After all, pleasure isn't evil in itself. Rather, it is the continual pursuit of pleasure at the expense of integrity, conviction, and responsibility that drive a person to destructive tendencies. You can represent the lighthouse both to parents and their young people that warns them of the dangers.

"But wait," you might say, "That sounds so dreary. Isn't there room for pleasure in our lives, even as adults?" Of course, the answer is, "Yes!" But pleasure can't be the goal. It's the byproduct of a mission-oriented life.

Mission doesn't mean all work and no play. It means balance where a focus on God and others deepen a person's life, where faith and service provide meaning, and where immediate gratification is replaced with the investment in the future. Youth ministry today must empower young people to contribute, not just receive.

At the age of 15, Brian was addicted to video games. He spent hours engrossed in play. His online community was a culture of its own. He missed meals, shunned relationships, and his schoolwork was suffering.

Brian needed a team approach to help him change. Parents, church leaders, and counselors came alongside this young man to help him. Resistance was high at first. Anger episodes increased, and tension dominated home life. But parents realized that allowing Brian to continue on his present course would contribute to his ultimate failure.

In order to reign in the brain stimulation that was now driving him, he needed help from several directions. Brian's support team initiated changes. One piece of the strategy was to target major beliefs in Brian's heart regarding pleasure. In honest moments, he was willing to admit he was out of balance and he didn't have the strength to get out of the cycle.

It's been a year now for Brian. It's been a rough road for family life as parents set limits and became more intentional with him. Here's what Brian said recently, "I realize that I can obtain that same positive feeling of getting to the next level now in more healthy ways. I work out. I help on the Audio Team at church. I'm doing better at school. When I achieve a goal I experience that same sense of accomplishment."

The Bible points young people to a pathway. It's the great adventure. You see spiritual forces at work, learn how you fit into the bigger plan of God, and receive internal affirmation of the Holy Spirit that you are on the right track. Major opportunities for advancement both internally and with others await the person willing to open his or her heart to God.

Your message to parents is important too. Many parents believe that "adolescence is a time to have fun," or "I want to give my child a better life than I had," or they excuse a permissive approach to adolescence by saying to themselves, "everyone else their age is doing it," or "my parenting job is to pull back and let them choose for themselves."

It's because of this principle that more and more churches are moving from an entertainment model for young people to a discipleship model. Church leaders are providing youth activities that are focused on service and personal spiritual growth, not just pleasure.

Focus on the heart, not just behavior. The high pressure to maintain image during adolescence is daunting. In fact, our culture seems to train young people to make a priority of what others see. Social media encourages "likes." Styles and appearance are essential. Grades, not performance, measure progress. In that environment, it becomes easy to neglect what's really important.

The heart is the central processing unit of a person. It's where emotions, desires, and beliefs generate attitudes, convictions, and character. When a person has inner strength, it affects all they do. If young people focus more on heart training instead of image management, they develop the muscles needed to meet the challenges of life.

The heart develops tendencies that become prepackaged responses. They're predictable. If you want to know what's in the heart of a person, watch their patterns. How do they respond to irritation, disappointment, interruption, accusation, or even correction? The young man who grunts, stomps, or throws insults when asked to stop the video game and help with groceries has a heart problem. The young woman who has an anger episode when corrected reveals the heart.

When young people recognize the heart's power, they can build the internal character necessary to face all kinds of challenges. Character can be defined as a pattern of thinking and acting in response to a challenge. The organized person thinks and acts differently than the disorganized person. The same is true with the person who is patient, gracious, or peaceful.

You want to continually call young people to look at and strengthen their hearts. When young people learn to value the heart, their whole world changes. That's why God chooses to live in the heart of a person. It's there He can reorganize values and build convictions. Proverbs 4:23 makes it clear, "Above all else, guard your heart, for everything you do flows from it" (NIV).

When church leaders grasp this idea then they naturally recalibrate their focus. Judy Wiles, a Children's Ministry Director says it this way:

> "I began to work in children's ministry after I found life in Christ in a new way some years ago. Before that time, I would work as a Sunday School teacher because I felt I should, and it was the right thing to do, and because I was pretty good with kids. After I came to grasp this life in Christ in a deeper way, I felt compelled to teach like I never had before.
>
> "For me, early on, no one talked about how life in Christ was about our hearts and minds shifting and transforming to be more Christ-like. It was like we gave our lives to Christ, and the rest was supposed to follow, but we weren't given any guidance. In my ministry, I began to see that much of the children's Sunday School curriculum was more works-based with little guidance as to what was going on in the heart, and how God designed us to learn and grow in Him."

Judy made the shift. Her ministry took on new passion. She continues to work with children but also partners with parents to reach the hearts. She says, "Just imagine what a generation of kids can accomplish for the kingdom if they grasp this heart-based approach to life, and embrace sanctification at an early age."

With some direction, many parents are willing to step up. Instead of delegating the responsibility of spiritual training to the church, they can recognize their part in the partnership.

Spiritual training of children is similar to driver education. There are two parts. The first part is in the classroom where kids learn about the facts, the principles and the rules about driving. The second part is the "behind the wheel" experience. In a similar way, children learn at home how to practice their faith. They learn how to make decisions that involve God's Word, manage their emotions under the power of the Holy Spirit, and they learn how to practice God's grace in daily relationships.

All parents are also on the road to find Christ and grow in Him. Their own weaknesses are often a challenge for a growing adolescent. Your work with young people and their parents is often a call to deeper discipleship for the whole family.

As you partner with parents and young people, you'll continually want to strengthen and empower the heart. The pressures kids face today are great. How will a young person meet the challenges of pornography, substance abuse, or materialism? The real solutions are deep and may not be reflected in good grades, a job, or manners. Your intentional and strategic work with parents and young people can go a long way to focus on the heart and help them with the underlying strength needed for life.

Teach young people how to use today's challenges to build life skills for the future. Dave, at age 21, is now working in his first real job. As he reflects on where he's come from he says this, "I like doing the work I was trained to do. But the biggest challenges in my job are the people I work with and the things they expect me to do with them after work. I have a much easier time than others saying no to their pressure. I'm sure that's because my parents helped me develop convictions. I didn't realize it as a teenager, but learning how to face temptations early helped me prepare for my life now."

Every situation faced by a young person becomes an opportunity to practice life skills for the future. This one idea helps young people gain much needed perspective on their lives right now. An angry coach, overwhelming assignments, and a friend's betrayal are all training exercises.

Elliot Lee taught twelve to fourteen year old boys in Sunday School. He called his meetings with them "strategy sessions." Elliot would invite the boys to share a challenge they were experiencing and then, as a group, they would brainstorm about solutions.

He said, "Too often kids make themselves out to be victims where their happiness depends on others. God's Word is empowering but it has to be relevant. I love to take Bible stories and apply them to problems kids are having right now. We talk about struggles with algebra, an absentee father, and getting kicked off the baseball team. I know that these conversations aren't just for the moment and to get through this week. I'm developing young men who will know how to face life in the future."

The church needs to be a place where God's Word meets life. Your leadership for parents and young people can provide that link. Adolescence is a time to learn how to cooperate with leadership, respond well to correction, and handle disappointment with grace. Kids need to know the "what," including facts about Bible stories and truths from God's Word. They also need to understand "how" so they can apply those truths to peers who attract them toward temptations, to teachers at school who mock Christianity, and to personal struggles they face every day.

As you work with young people you want to communicate this essential message: Adolescence is about practice, preparation, and training and God's Word is the instruction manual. The home you live in is not an accident. The siblings you interact with, the parents you respond to, and the house you live in, are all training opportunities. Relational and school challenges need solutions now that will transfer to your future as well.

During adolescence parents must exert more parental control where life skills don't yet exist. This idea is often counter-intuitive if parents are trying to help their kids become more independent. Unfortunately independence without character leads to disaster.

Larry is a family pastor and took a proactive role with Sam and his mom. Mom told him, "When my kids hit thirteen-years-old, it's time for them to learn to sink or swim. I pull back and they need to manage themselves." Her great idea worked with the older two, but now her fourteen-year-old Sam was failing at school, using anger as a weapon in the home, and burying himself in electronics.

Mom has a good idea. In fact her idea is great. But Larry helped Mom see that Sam needed a different good idea. He was not internally motivated to do much of anything that required work. Thus, Mom needed to adjust her thinking and provide more parental control. Sam needed more structure and accountability to develop the life skills necessary for his success. Larry provided just what Mom needed to help adjust her thinking because of her son's needs.

Your message about building life skills now brings more purpose to the chaos of young people's lives and gives them hope. It also opens the door for you to provide parents with direction.

Help young people bring their salvation into each new stage of development. Two factors contribute to the disintegration of faith during the adolescent years. First is the early emphasis on faith facts without practical application, and second is not experiencing God in new ways as a child passes through developmental stages. Both weaken faith so much that young people often feel like they've grown out of faith now that they are moving toward adulthood.

227

To prevent faith from becoming a mist that disappears over time, it's essential that you show young people how to practice their faith today. They can't live on yesterday's faith for very long without feeling its weakening effects.

Adolescence is a time of fast-paced growth. The pressure and challenges of life can be daunting. Physical, mental, and emotional energy is taxed daily at a high rate. When spirituality remains at the center, young people can face life with confidence. Your work to help young people grow into their relationship with Christ is essential.

The experiential side of the gospel takes the truths of God's Word and sees them useful in the moment. Rose, a high school mentor, focused on prayer with Kayla, who at age 15, experienced a dramatic change in her spirituality.

Kayla reported it this way.

"My prayers used to emphasize what I wanted from God. I would ask for help on a test, a sunny day for my soccer game, or for my parents to say yes to my request. When all went well, I would feel like God was listening. But there were a lot of times that God didn't give me what I wanted. So, I felt like God didn't care about me because He didn't answer my prayers. So I stopped praying.

"Then I learned from Rose that I was praying the wrong way. I want to hear God speak. I want to have a close relationship with Him, but my approach to prayer was getting in the way. Now I pray differently. I ask God how I can fit into His plans. It's not about my desires but rather me partnering with what God is doing.

"It's been so helpful for me to pray this way each morning. It makes me more sensitive to what God is doing. When I see that someone is sad, I wonder if God wants me to offer encouragement. When I experience disappointment I ask God what He wants me to learn in this situation. God is more real to me now than ever. As I read the Bible He speaks to me and I'm learning to listen to His voice."

You can do a lot to help young people recognize the value of their spiritual lives. You might ask your students, "What is God saying to you today? I'd like to know because I think God wants to speak to me through you." Too often the emphasis in children and youth ministry is that kids are the receivers and that teachers are the givers. This approach often leads to spiritual passivity.

Christianity is practical for young people. Encouraging them to experience God on a daily basis creates more depth to their theological experience. Trying out and testing the armor of God or mustard seed faith can propel spiritual growth. Learning to trust God over peers, teachers, or even their own thoughts is powerful.

But what if a young person isn't interested in spiritual things? A young person's interest in spiritual things isn't a prerequisite for good teaching or parenting. Balancing relationship with truth is essential, and shying away from either can be detrimental.

The above four principles are a recalibration of thinking for young people. They aren't just biblical truths; they're life-changing principles. Parents and church leaders must be willing to use more than dialogue to bring about change in the resistant child. You can help parents embrace other tools such as firmness, visioning, structure, consequences, teaching, and coaching.

But all tools are enhanced when they contain a flavor of the gospel. The home and the church partner together by using a multi-faceted approach designed to impact a child's heart. You and parents may have some good ideas, but any particular child may need different methods. It's in those moments that a child's unique needs often require an individualized strategy.

As you look for ways to influence young people, keep the mission in mind. When you focus on these four principles, they form a road map for making your youth ministry most effective.

The primary goal of youth ministry is to train young people to be disciples of Jesus Christ and to empower their parents to equip them. You'll want to use relationship and activities as vehicles to communicate a higher purpose for the current stage of life. The goal is not just to help them survive the teen years, but to help them thrive in life.

Measuring the New Norm

Honest evaluation of the following questions will help you measure your success. These points will also give you greater passion and direction to reach the goal.

- Are young people coming to church eager to serve?
- What ways are you providing for young people to serve?
- What activities are employed calling young people to discipleship? How do your activities show them discipleship?
- How are young people discovering that the Bible is relevant and practical for their lives?
- What are the methods you are using to impart vision to young people that their current faith experience is preparation for bigger things in the future?
- In what ways are young people communicating their faith in experiential ways by initiating their own prayer life, Bible study, and listening to God?
- What reports are you hearing from home and elsewhere about how young people are building a Christ-centered life?
- What type of equipping times are you utilizing for parents to learn, share, and explore biblical parenting strategies? How often are you providing these opportunities?

Resources to Explore Further

Dr. Scott Turansky and Joanne Miller are the founders of the National Center for Biblical Parenting. They help parents use a heart-based approach with children of all ages and empower churches to equip them. They have written 15 books on parenting, train coaches to work one-on-one with parents, and conduct live parenting seminars to help churches develop their parent discipleship programs.

One resource you might consider is the THRIVE! Family Video Experience for small group or family use. You will find the book *Parenting is Heart Work* to be foundational. Their website is www. biblicalparenting.org.

- *Limited Church, Unlimited Kingdom* by Rob Rienow
- *The Family Friendly Church* by Ben Freudenberg
- *Parenting Unchained: Overcoming the Ten Deceptions That Shackle Christian Parents* by Dr. James D. Dempsey

Randall House would like to say a special

Thank You

to the following contributors for their work on this project:

Tammy G. Daughtry	*Philip Nation*
Brian Haynes	*Jim Putman*
Ron Hunter Jr.	*Lydia Randall*
Timothy Paul Jones	*Richard Ross*
Scott Kedersha	*Jay Strother*
Joanne Miller	*Scott Turansky*
Jimmy Myers	*Jim Wideman*
	Christopher Yuan

All royalties from this book will go to support D6 International. To date, the D6 Conference has been held in the following countries: France, Malaysia, Norway, Singapore, and South Korea. The annual D6 Conferences equip ministers and families in generational discipleship and Randall House supports these countries in providing graphic design, themes, speakers, videos, and resources.

Contributors

Tammy G. Daughtry is a national advocate for kids in complex families. She is the author of *Co-parenting Works, Helping Children Thrive after Divorce*, and the executive director of the digital resource, "One Heart, Two Homes." Tammy speaks about what kids need when parents are raising them after a divorce, in a stepfamily, or when parents are not married. Focus on the Family and FamilyLife Radio are just a few of the 50+ media outlets she has been featured on.

Brian Haynes, D.Min. serves as lead pastor for Bay Area Church and is a writer and frequent speaker focused on renovating people, families, and churches. Dr. Haynes is best known for his work in family ministry and generational discipleship and most recently co-authored the book *Relentless Parenting: The Crucial Pursuit of Your Teen's Heart*, with his wife, Angela. Together they have three daughters and live in Houston, Texas.

Ron Hunter Jr., Ph.D. is the CEO of Randall House (publisher of D6 Curriculum—D6 is an abbreviation for Deuteronomy 6). Dr. Hunter is the author or coauthor of three books, *The DNA of D6: Building Blocks of Generational Discipleship, Youth Ministry in the 21st Century: 5 Views*, and *Toy Box Leadership*. He is the cofounder and director of the D6 Conference, but his favorite titles are husband and father.

Timothy Paul Jones, Ph.D. is professor of family ministry and apologetics at The Southern Baptist Theological Seminary; he also serves as a pastor at Sojourn Community Church. Jones has authored or edited more than a dozen books in the fields of apologetics and family ministry, including *Family Ministry Field Guide*, and award-winners *Christian History Made Easy*, and *How We Got the Bible*. His passion is to equip churches and parents with the tools they need to instill resilient faith in their children.

Scott Kedersha is the director of marriage ministry at Watermark Community Church, where he has served on the marriage team since 2006. Through Watermark's marriage ministry he has helped prepare nearly-weds, establish newlyweds, and enrich and restore all marriages. His first book, *Ready or Knot?*, came out earlier this year with Baker Books. He lives in the Dallas area with his wife and four sons. Learn more at www.scottkedersha.com.

Joanne Miller, RN, BSN is one of the founders of the National Center for Biblical Parenting. She has a passion for equipping parents and grandparents with a heart-based approach to parenting. Joanne and her husband, Ed, have two grown sons, a daughter-in-law, and two grandchildren. Joanne is a pediatric nurse, author, and speaker.

Jimmy Myers, Ph.D. is the co-owner/CEO of the Timothy Center. A multi-campus Christian counseling facility in Austin, Texas. He founded the Timothy Center after serving 20 years as a youth minister in the local church. He is also a speaker, author, and podcast host. His latest book, co-authored by George Barna, is entitled *Fearless Parenting: How to Raise Faithful Kids in a Secular Culture*. The marriage and family-related podcast that he co-hosts with his son, Josh, can be found at pairadocspodcast.com.

Philip Nation, D.Min. is a ministry leader, professor, and author. He serves as the Director of Global Impact Churches for the Baptist World Alliance and as an assistant professor with Houston Baptist University. He is the author of several books and Bible studies including *Habits for Our Holiness* on missional spirituality, *Storm Shelter* on the Psalms, and *Pursuing Holiness: Applications from James*. He is overjoyed to be married to Angie and the father of two sons, Andrew and Chris. He blogs at philipnation.net.

Jim Putman is the co-founder and senior pastor of Real Life Ministries in Post Falls, Idaho. Jim holds degrees from Boise State University and Boise Bible College. He is the author of three books: *Church Is a Team Sport*, *Real-Life Discipleship*, and *The Power of Together*, and co-author of *DiscipleShift* and *Hope For The Prodigal*. Jim's passion is discipleship through small groups. He and his wife, along with their three sons, daughters-in-law, and four grandchildren, live in scenic North Idaho.

Lydia Randall is a wife and mother who has been serving parents and children for over two decades through her ministry with Lake Pointe Church in Rockwall, Texas. Lydia serves as the director of HomePointe and is the creator of the Faith Path strategy. Lydia is the author of *My Faith Box*. She spearheads cross-divisional strategies for creating a culture of intentional families at Lake Pointe and beyond with HomePointe Inc. Lydia also serves as the women's chaplain for the Texas Rangers baseball team.

Richard Ross, Ph.D. is husband to LaJuana, who has joined him in a lifetime of loving teenagers. They are parents of Clayton. Richard served as youth minister for thirty years and now is a volunteer with teenagers and parents at Wedgwood Baptist in Fort Worth. Richard is professor to the next generation of youth ministers at Southwestern Seminary in Fort Worth. Since its inception, Richard has served as the spokesperson for the international True Love Waits movement. He has written 23 books for youth leaders and parents and speaks in over 35 conferences and churches each year.

Jay Strother is the pastor of The Church at Station Hill, a regional campus of Brentwood (TN) Baptist Church where he previously served as the NextGen minister. He's the author of *Loving Well: Healthy Relationships*, a contributing author to *Perspectives on Family Ministry* and many other NextGen resources. His favorite stories come from 21 years of marriage, three daughters, and a son adopted from Nepal. Jay enjoys good books, long hikes, strong coffee, and St. Louis Cardinals baseball.

Scott Turansky, D.Min. and his wife, Carrie, have five children and six grandchildren. He is the co-founder of the National Center for Biblical Parenting. Scott has a passion for equipping parents, grandparents, and church leaders with a heart-based approach to help children thrive. Scott is a professor at Concordia University and he trains coaches to work with parents through Biblical Parenting University, the online Parent Training Center. He is also an author and a pastor.

Jim Wideman is considered a pioneer and one of the fathers of the family ministry movement. He is an Orange Strategist and thinker with over 40 years of hands-on experience in the local church. Jim currently serves as the family pastor at The Belonging Company in Nashville, Tennessee. Jim and his wife have two daughters and two of the most handsome grandsons ever born!

Christopher Yuan, D.Min. has taught the Bible at Moody Bible Institute for over ten years and his speaking ministry on faith and sexuality has reached five continents. He speaks at conferences, on college campuses, and in churches. He has co-authored with his mother their memoir (now in seven languages), *Out of a Far Country: A Gay Son's Journey to God, A Broken Mother's Search for Hope* and he is also the author of *Giving a Voice to the Voiceless*. Christopher graduated from Moody Bible Institute in 2005, Wheaton College Graduate School in 2007 with a Master of Arts in Biblical Exegesis, and received his doctorate of ministry in 2014 from Bethel Seminary. Dr. Yuan's newest book is *Holy Sexuality and the Gospel: Sex, Desire, and Relationships Shaped by God's Grand Story.*

What is **D6**?

BASED ON DEUTERONOMY 6:4-7

A **conference** for your entire **team**

A **curriculum** for every age at **church**

An **experience** for every person in your **home**

Connecting
CHURCH & HOME
These must work together!

DEFINE & REFINE Your Discipleship Plan

www.d6family.com